The Historical Imagination:
Postmodernism and the Treatment of the Past in Contemporary British Fiction

FREDERICK M. HOLMES

The Historical Imagination: Postmodernism and the Treatment of the Past in Contemporary British Fiction

English Literary Studies
University of Victoria
1997

ENGLISH LITERARY STUDIES
Published at the University of Victoria

Founding Editor
Samuel L. Macey

GENERAL EDITOR
Robert M. Schuler

EDITORIAL BOARD
Thomas R. Cleary
Evelyn M. Cobley
Kathryn Kerby-Fulton
Stephen A. C. Scobie
Nelson C. Smith

ADVISORY EDITORS
David Fowler, *University of Washington*
Donald Greene, *University of Southern California*
Juliet McMaster, *University of Alberta*
Richard J. Schoeck, *University of Colorado*
Arthur Sherbo, *Michigan State University*

BUSINESS MANAGER
Hedy Miller

ISBN 0-920604-53-6 ✓

The ELS Monograph Series is published in consultation with members of the Department by ENGLISH LITERARY STUDIES, Department of English, University of Victoria, P.O. Box 3070, Victoria, B.C., Canada, v8w 3w1.

ELS Monograph Series No. 73
© 1997 by Frederick M. Holmes
Cover art: Mark Nisenholt

For Pat

CONTENTS

ACKNOWLEDGMENTS

Some of the research for this book was made possible by an award from the Research Projects Fund of The Social Sciences and Humanities Research Council of Canada.

Portions of this study have been published elsewhere in somewhat different form. I have reworked parts of the following articles: "The Representation of History as Plastic: The Search for the Real Thing in Graham Swift's *Ever After*," *Ariel* 27.3 (1996): 25-43; "The Historical Imagination and the Victorian Past: A. S. Byatt's *Possession*," *English Studies in Canada* 20 (1994): 319-34; "History, Fiction, and the Dialogic Imagination: John Fowles's *A Maggot*," *Contemporary Literature* 32 (1991): 229-43. I wish to thank the editors and publishers of the journals listed for granting permission to use material from these articles.

I would like to thank my editor, Robert Schuler, for his intelligent copy-editing and for his overall helpfulness and efficiency.

While working on this project, I have benefited from the opportunity to present and listen to papers at the University of Louisville's annual Twentieth-Century Literature Conference. I wish to acknowledge the young academics who shared their ideas with me there. I particularly wish to thank Bruce Lord, John Marsden, Nicola Pitchford, Dana Shiller, Debra Raschke, Michael Trussler, and Lynn Wells.

I have profited from extensive discussions of my ideas with my colleague Kim Fedderson, who shares my enthusiastic interest in jazz and pool.

My greatest debt is to my family. My stepson, Paul Jasen, shares my interest in postmodernism. My wife, Patricia Jasen, has been unstinting in her emotional and intellectual support. Her ideas on how to improve the manuscript were invaluable. This book is dedicated to her.

INTRODUCTION

Theoretical Considerations

A cook in Napoleon's army; Thomas Chatterton, the eighteenth-century forger of medieval texts; a pair of Victorian poets engaged in a clandestine love affair; an eighteenth-century prostitute who becomes a religious visionary; a writer of British propaganda during the Second World War who has witnessed some of the most significant events of the first half of the twentieth century—these are some of the characters in a group of novels which participate in the much-discussed return to history in contemporary literature and criticism. These particular novels have in common an intent not just to delight readers with fascinating characters and compelling stories from earlier eras but also to stimulate an interest in the methods by which we know the past and the uses to which we put that knowledge. As a result, these works have a propensity to comment self-consciously upon the historical material which they dramatize. Linda Hutcheon describes this phenomenon succinctly in coining the term "historiographic metafiction" to denote "novels which are both intensely self-reflexive and yet paradoxically also lay claim to historical events and personages" (*Poetics* 5). The paradox inheres in the way that such works create a vivid illusion of the unfolding of historical events, involving people who actually existed, only to dispel the illusion by laying bare the artifices that give rise to it. In contrast, traditional historical novels sustain throughout the pretence of supplying direct access to the past in all of its fullness and particularity. Such novels employ the methods of formal realism, such as "solidity of specification," to combine as seamlessly as possible wholly fictional ingredients with information garnered from actual historical sources. As Brian McHale says, whereas traditional historical novels "typically involve some violation of ontological boundaries," they "strive to suppress these violations, to hide the ontological 'seams' between fictional projections and real world facts." It is, of course, just these "seams" which postmodern historical fiction is intent to flaunt (16-17).

This book is a critical study of several British novels, written over the past decade or so, which purport to narrate portions of the historical past while also paradoxically exhibiting their "seams"; in the process, they not only expose the thinness of fictional illusion but also say

11

something about the difficulties of all attempts to investigate and represent experience. All of the works are, to one degree or another and according to one definition or another, postmodernist. Since postmodern historical fiction is being written in English in many countries, including my own, Canada, I confess to being somewhat arbitrary in not considering novels such as Timothy Findley's *Famous Last Words* and Michael Ondaatje's *The English Patient*. But there is some justification for restricting attention to British examples beyond the fact that my primary focus in teaching and research is twentieth-century British literature. Both Patricia Waugh and Alison Lee have identified a unifying factor in pointing out that British postmodern fiction, although subversive of the realist tradition of the novel, tends to be more closely attached to that tradition than is avant-garde fiction written elsewhere (Waugh, *Metafiction* 49; Lee xii). Rather than attempting an exhaustive survey of British "historiographic metafiction," I have focused most of my attention on the following eight novels, some of which I alluded to in my opening sentence: *A Maggot* by John Fowles, *Chatterton* by Peter Ackroyd, *Star Turn* by Nigel Williams, *The Passion* by Jeanette Winterson, *A History of the World in 10 1/2 Chapters* by Julian Barnes, *Possession* by A. S. Byatt, *Moon Tiger* by Penelope Lively, and *Ever After* by Graham Swift. Restricting most of my attention to these eight might appear to be a somewhat artificial constraint, but I believe that it is justified by the need to provide enough textual detail for critical analysis to be meaningful. This strategy has allowed me to treat each work extensively enough to do some justice to its artistic richness and individuality, and at the same time to consider a sufficient number of works to make it meaningful to point out family resemblances and differences—to make it possible, in other words, to generalize about an evolving sub-genre.

I mentioned that the renewed interest in history apparent in recent literature is shared by contemporary literary criticism and theory. One anxiety common to both the novels listed and critical theory is the suspicion that history is fundamentally discontinuous and therefore incommunicable. It might simply be delusive to think that a real understanding of a determinate, continuous past can be gained by empirical means. And if history is radically discontinuous, if, as David Perkins categorically states, "[h]istorical interpretations and explanations cannot themselves transcend the time and place in which they are produced" (*Is Literary History Possible?* 16), then is knowledge of the past possible at all in any real sense? Many contemporary novelists and theorists grapple with this problem of historicism, the sceptical view that objective knowledge of history is impossible because knowledge itself is the product of history. Michel Foucault is the most prominent debunker of a unified view of history, but according to Robert D'Amico, Foucault himself never overcomes the challenge of historicism. He has no grounds on which to dismiss the empiricism and teleology of the traditional history of ideas, for if changes in knowledge do not amount to progress, then how can Foucault's criticisms be other than arbitrary (92)? "If all thought is a prisoner of its contemporaneous episteme or all commentary merely description, how can there be criticism?" (94). For Louis Montrose, no explanation or commentary can ever be disinterested or untainted by ideology. The truth of all assertions about history is necessarily relative to the gender, ethnicity, class, age and profession of the would-be commentator (29-30). A central aim of this book is to explore the effects of such relativism on the representation of history in the group of novels which I have chosen.

One quite understandable effect of the tendency of contemporary fiction to incorporate historical subject matter is a blurring of the distinction between history and literature. This phenomenon has led to challenging theoretical questions about the relationship between history and literature. Is recorded history a stabilizing context against which literary texts can be understood, or, as Tony Bennett asks, is history itself composed of representations which are no different in their dependence on narrative and rhetoric from the literature for which they would serve as a ground? If the answer to the second question is yes, then, as Bennett goes on to say, as an "effect of discourse itself, [history] is unable to function as an extra-discursive source of anything else" (52). As Dominick LaCapra argues, historical contexts are inferences made on the basis of particular texts, not separable realities which pre-exist and anchor those texts: "The difficulties in the process of inferentially reconstructing contexts on the basis of texts . . . are often obscured or repressed, especially when one is convinced that a context or set of contexts must be a determinative force with full explanatory power" (128). In the words of Fredric Jameson, "history is inaccessible to us except in textual form . . . [and] it can be approached only by way of prior (re)textualization" (*Political Unconscious* 82). Opposed to formalism though they be, critics of a materialist stripe, such as Bennett and Jameson, have not found it easy to extricate themselves from the quagmire of textuality in order to establish an unproblematic connection with social reality.

This is not a work of critical theory, although, as will already be apparent, it draws eclectically on the insights of theorists from a variety of schools. If we substitute theory in general for a very loosely defined structuralism, David Lodge expresses my intentions in desiring "to work with structuralism, not only in the sense of applying it when it seems useful to do so, but also in the sense of working *alongside* it, recognizing its existence as a fact of intellectual life without being totally dominated by it" (viii). For me, not being dominated by it means, among other things, reserving the right to retain what could be crudely characterized as liberal humanist assumptions, suitably qualified and tailored to current circumstances, when I believe that the challenges to those positions are overstated or otherwise less than compelling. It is germane in this regard that according to some of its theorists postmodernism itself is supposed to entail not an outright rejection but a critical recasting of traditional post-Enlightenment concepts and practices, such as individuality or rationality or empiricism (Hutcheon, *Poetics* 19). And yet in practice, what tends to be emphasized, depending on whether or not the theorist's politics makes him or her favourably disposed toward postmodernism, is either its welcome critique of a benighted humanism (Lyotard 81-82; Lee 57; Spanos 2-3) or its lamentable complicity in the cultural commodification of late capitalism (Graff 94-95; Jameson, *Postmodernism* x; Eagleton, *Ideology* 373). Although Hutcheon herself has disclaimed any intention to take sides in the controversy over postmodernism (*Poetics* ix), it seems to me that implicitly her work champions the radical claims of this multifaceted phenomenon. Features of contemporary culture and literature which do not square with *a priori* definitions of postmodernism are often ignored by critics, and sometimes those features bespeak a positive continuity with, rather than a parodic or ironic reworking of, earlier traditions. I hope that by not trying to make the particular objects of my study fit a prefabricated general definition of postmodernism I have been better able to apprehend their intricacies and to show the respects in which they travel against the current of expectations formed by contemporary theory.

An example of the sort of interpretation which I have tried to avoid is Alison Lee's assertion in her reading of *Hawksmoor* that the metaphysical dimension of Ackroyd's metafictional gothic tale can be discounted. The novel seems to hold out the possibility that a transcendent power of evil is behind the repetition in the twentieth century of a series of early eighteenth-century sacrificial murders perpetrated by the Satan-worshipping architect Nicholas Dyer as secret, unholy rites to commemorate the building of several London churches that were intended to replace ones destroyed in the Great Fire of 1666 (the symbolic significance of the last three digits is not lost on him) (*Hawksmoor* 144). Yet because Lee's concept of postmodernism (which is an amalgam of the thinking of, amongst others, Foucault, Althusser, Benveniste, Barthes, and Derrida) denies in advance the possibility of transcendent identities or origins, she states that "a foray into the spirit world would imply a human essence, and *Hawksmoor* disputes this as either a spiritual or a literary possibility" (72). But is it the novel which categorically forecloses on this interpretive option, or is it the ideology of the critic? Lee cleverly explicates the novel's self-reflexive tendency to dissolve its patterns of significance in an ambiguous, unrestricted play of textuality, but equally pervasive are contradictory references which ground the novel's reality in the corruption of the earth, in the certainty of death, and in the ubiquitous evil inherent in existence. It might even be possible to reconcile the countervailing factors if we see the transcendent power not as an essential source of human identity, but as the force that negates it and disperses potentially positive meanings along a chain of shadowy differences. Viewed in this way, *Hawksmoor*'s representation of evil can be seen to follow in the tradition of canonized precursors such as Milton and Conrad. Rather than being contradicted by the "notness" which, Lee claims (83), defines the postmodern, an idealist metaphysics might at least be considered as a way to account for the vertiginous qualities of *Hawksmoor*, in view of evidence that can be adduced from the text itself.

As I hope the above reading suggests, my method in this study has been empirical in attending to the concrete particulars of the novels, but I do not argue that my ability to see those details, let alone sometimes to arrange them into patterns, is independent of disciplinary contexts which already involve historically contingent interpretations. In other words, I eschew a foundationalist posture and embrace pluralism and relativism, although I *am* making determinate assertions which, I hope, are backed by persuasive reasoning. Even though I do not claim any special authority for my views, the desire to formulate stable and coherent meanings, even of a provisional kind, might seem ironically inappropriate. Might not this critical goal be viewed as a penchant for totalization in an indeterminate and weightless postmodern world of dislocated simulacra, given that the novels in question all feature a good deal of scepticism about their own capacity to represent the objective reality of the past? Must not any criticism dealing with them run afoul of the same problem of legitimation which renders them irresolutely self-conscious and which is, according to Jean-François Lyotard, an effect of the "incredulity toward metanarratives" that defines the postmodern condition (xxiv)?

15

My answer is that, if one allows for the differences between narrative fiction and analytical literary criticism, the novels are like my discourse about them in also making, in a contingent way and from limited perspectives, determinate statements of one kind or another about various matters. The points at which they display a general epistemological scepticism do not cancel these meanings because, as Stanley Fish says, "one does not doubt in a vacuum but from a perspective, and that perspective is itself immune to doubt until it has been replaced by another which will then be similarly immune" (360). Broad scepticism, in other words, issues from particular experiences that confer a base of knowledge, however shortlived. The books bear out Fish's contention that the "project of radical doubt can never outrun the necessity of being situated; in order to doubt *everything*, including the ground one stands on, one must stand somewhere else, and that somewhere else will then be the ground on which one stands" (360). Even if total scepticism were a possibility—which it obviously is not because it precludes asserting anything, including scepticism—it would still constitute, in the words of Gerald Graff, "a kind of *understanding* of the way things really are" (11).

Of course, I recognize the circularity of what I am here proposing generally about the novels' meanings, since I confess that any comments which I make about those texts already involve interpretations and do not stand as pre-interpretive objective descriptions of them. I accept that to one degree or another readers constitute what they read and that, for a host of individual and broadly cultural reasons, different readers often "see" the same text in markedly different ways. That said, however, the discipline does supply criteria, tied to particular critical orientations and methodologies, which allow us to judge some interpretations superior in some ways to others. I can, therefore, hope that my readings and the assumptions upon which they are based will prove convincing.

I also hope that the structural building blocks and boundaries of this book will establish themselves as valid and useful, if not as unshakably solid and impermeable, at a time when conceptual categories and distinctions are shifting and dissolving with an alarming fluidity under the pressure of postmodern theory. In restricting the field of my attention to novels, for example, I am open to the same charge which Steven Connor levels against McHale's *Postmodernist Fiction*: that it "is characterized by a serene belief in the givenness of the category of literature" and that it treats the literary as "an unanalysed or unanalysable blank, or as an elastic frame which expands obediently to contain every kind of

16

subversion" (126). I would answer that literature is, in rough and ready terms, distinct. The boundaries which provide this distinctness *are* remarkably elastic and permeable not because of literature's ontological integrity as an entity or its immunity from the coercions of ideology, but precisely because literature is culturally produced and subject to historical changes. One does not have to claim that it has an essential, static, autonomous nature in order to isolate it for attention or to explore its internal dynamics. The readiness of much contemporary fiction to blur the distinction between its inside and outside, to open itself in dialogic fashion to the welter of other discourses, does not obscure the fact that these works are being written, published, written about, catalogued in libraries, and taught as novels rather than something else. John Updike, for example, may castigate the textually hybrid *Flaubert's Parrot* for not sufficiently conforming to traditional expectations of what a novel should look like and do, but he is never in any doubt that it is as a novel that Julian Barnes's work should be reviewed (86-87).

And, despite the attempts by writers of fiction to confound generic distinctions between novels and other kinds of writing, there might be internal as well as the aforementioned external, institutional factors which, at least to an extent, set these works off as literature. I implied as much earlier in claiming artistic distinction for the books to be discussed and in expressing the desire to communicate something of their richness as novels. Whether the aesthetic qualities of which I speak reside in the works themselves or whether they are products of particular strategies of reading is admittedly difficult to determine, but it seems probable that there is a reciprocal relationship between conventions of reading and the intrinsic features of those works which communicate intentions. Again, though, what prevents the making of objective descriptions of those inherent properties is the fact that our experience of them, which leads to the fashioning of new conventions, is already mediated by pre-existing interpretive frameworks. That qualification aside, it still seems possible to say that the identity of literature is determined by internal as well as external, contextual factors.

Reactionary though his *The Pleasures of Reading in an Ideological Age* might be as a recipe for criticism, Robert Alter seems justified, therefore, in arguing for the identity of "intrinsically literary values" that are synonymous with "the pleasure [literature] gives us as we experience the nice interplay between the verbal aesthetic form and the complex meanings conveyed" (28). Alter does not, of course, claim that such an interplay is absent from many non-literary texts or that historically the distinction between what is and is not literature has been absolute or

17

unchanging (48). Nor does he aver that the literary canon has been immune to the influence of political ideologies (26), although he also makes a convincing case against the crude position of some politically engaged critics that the canon always serves society's dominant ideology (31).

While Alter might be right in saying that what identifies works from divergent times and places as literature are the aesthetic qualities that emerge from various kinds of verbal and generic patterning, and that a general cohesiveness is produced because writers tend to look to the past for models to emulate or rebel against, he is less persuasive in arguing that "this backward-looking aspect . . . cuts across political systems" (27). A given writer, it is true, can be captivated by the works of an earlier figure even when their political beliefs are in conflict, but if Alter means that the aesthetic is the part of literature that is exempt from the impurity of ideological struggle, then he is on shakier ground. Aesthetic phenomena are as subject to historical change as are any other aspects of culture. As a familiarity with literary traditions in the West discloses, all works can be seen to have aesthetic properties, but different kinds of properties are valued in different epochs. Aesthetic criteria and the relations they posit amongst authors, readers, texts, and society alter with time. One does not have to agree with all the particulars of Terry Eagleton's Marxist analysis in order to accept that the aesthetic can be the site of changing ideological struggles which are highly complex, unstable, and ambiguous (*Ideology of the Aesthetic*). As even the far-from-radical Wayne Booth states, "the effort to distinguish a domain of experience called the 'aesthetic' . . . led to hundreds of efforts to reconcile the drive for pure form with an experience that always revealed, on a close look, elements of moral and ideological engagement" (18).

My point in mentioning that aesthetic values are not wholly separate from political influences is not to create the misleading impression that my readings of the novels which I have selected will be dominated by political considerations. While I accept that everything has a political dimension, including aesthetics, I do not share the Marxist propensity to project the political dimension everywhere, or invidiously to equate novels which could be branded as postmodernist with the most ephemeral aesthetic commodities of late capitalism. It seems fairly obvious that aesthetic matters may also be bound up intimately with other kinds of concerns, be they ethical or psychological or religious, which are equally historically contingent and may be just as relevant for my purposes. I am interested in the relationship between the formal characteristics of the

18

narratives and their broadly historical engagement with a variety of life's aspects.

It remains for me in this introduction to explain very briefly the organization of the book as a whole and to introduce the topics to be explored. I have divided the work into five chapters corresponding to the following broad topics: (1) the relationship between historical significance and narrative patterning in the novels; (2) textual fragmentation, the proliferation of genres, and the dialogic nature of history; (3) the models or theories of history and the attitudes towards them which underlie the formal choices discussed in the first two chapters; (4) the relationship between history and subjectivity implied by the novels; (5) the status of artistic imagination posited by the novels in relation to the representation of history. The approach which I have chosen has enabled me to emphasize the common intellectual problems, themes, and technical matters relating to the novels' treatment of history. I trust that, in considering how they answer some of the important cultural challenges of our time, I have also been able to communicate something of the diversity and individuality of the eight books.

CHAPTER ONE

Historical Significance and Narrative Patterning

My first chapter examines the various ways in which the novels acknowledge, in their very shapes and attributes as narratives, that the representation of history is an enterprise fraught with difficulties and ambiguities. In one way or another all of the works display the kind of self-consciousness which, as Alter shows, breeds doubt about their own ontological status by "draw[ing] our attention to fictional form as a consciously articulated entity rather than a transparent container of 'real' events" (*Partial Magic* x). What is thereby called into question is not merely their own fictitiousness as invented stories rather than transcriptions of historical reality but, more significantly, the representational capacity of all narratives, even those which claim fidelity to fact. These novels correspond to the kind of modern historical discourse characterized by Hayden White as being highly suspicious of narrative and its emplotments: "Insofar as historical stories can be completed, can be given narrative closure, can be shown to have had a *plot* all along, they give to reality the odor of the *ideal*. This is why the plot of a historical narrative is always an embarrassment, and has to be presented as 'found' in the events rather than put there by narrative techniques" ("Value of Narrativity" 24). A way in which postmodern novelists, unlike traditional historians, can counteract this embarrassment is not by naturalizing plots but by disclosing through parody or some other means that they are perfectly aware that such coherence-generating patterns are simply fabrications.

For example, the overly intricate comic plot of *Possession* and the overly episodic and farcical treatment in *Star Turn* of the received "plots" of twentieth-century European history undermine, in opposite ways, the potential significance of these stories. Byatt's novel features separate plot strands involving, on the one hand, the nineteenth-century poets Randolph Ash and Christabel LaMotte and, on the other, Roland Michell and Maud Bailey, the twentieth-century academics who have discovered letters detailing the previously unknown love affair between the Victorian pair. This trove of documents is the source material which the modern scholars use to construct a historical narrative. What Maud and Roland learn from the secret love letters written by Randolph and Christabel, many of which the novel prints in full, is supplemented for the reader in sections set in the nineteenth century which further develop the relationship of the Victorian lovers. The nineteenth- and twentieth-century plot strands at first run parallel to one another and then converge. As they follow the faint traces of the Victorian poets through Yorkshire and Brittany, Roland and Maud eventually begin to experience the same sort of intellectual and emotional intimacy that Randolph and Christabel enjoy. The modern pair discover the identity and fate of their predecessors' illegitimate child, who unifies the narrative even more tightly by proving to have been Maud's great-great-great-grandmother.

Making the ending itself a point of origin, these previously hidden ties of kinship are a pointedly anachronistic device for providing closure. As more than one of the novel's reviewers noted, the melodramatic last part especially seems to belong in a Victorian rather than a contemporary novel (Shilling; Jenkyns 214). The villainous Mortimer Cropper, the American biographer of Ash, is apprehended during a savage thunder storm in the ghoulish act of digging up the grave of Ash and his wife, Ellen, in order to obtain the box of momentos which she had buried with them. The ensuing festive denouement, in which characters are rewarded and love triumphs, reminds us that the novel's subtitle is *A Romance*. Measured against the expectations of realism, this conclusion is, as Anita Brookner puts it, "almost impertinently unconvincing." The effect of its being parodically overdetermined is to deny readers the full measure of satisfaction that the ending of such a romance narrative could otherwise give. Intricate fictional plots which do not subvert themselves as Byatt's novel does could be interpreted as implying metaphorically the existence of a providential historical design in human affairs. Or (as Byatt herself asserts of the great nineteenth-century novels [*Passions* 167]) such narratives could be read as substitutes for a divine plot in which people no longer believe. In either interpretation, plots of this sort offer readers a comfort which *Possession* denies them.

Star Turn takes a different tack in undermining the notion that the plots of history exist in some natural form independent of the fabricated patterns of those who write the historical record. Williams's picaresque novel fragments the history of the first half of the twentieth century, thus rendering discontinuous the familiar, seamless narrative of the popular imagination in which the devastation of the First World War causes economic and political upheavals. These in turn threaten Western democracies (both from within and without) and eventually lead to the Second World War. In the British version of this story, heroism and collective sacrifice enable the nation to triumph over Kaisar Wilhelm's imperialism and aggression, and ultimately help to save the world from the evil of Hitler's Naziism. Owing to the pragmatic good sense of its political traditions, Britain rejects the radical (and disastrous) solutions adopted between the wars in other parts of the world; hence it resists internal threats to democracy posed by figures such as the fascist Oswald Mosley. Williams exposes this story as nationalistic myth-making, stripping it of dignity by treating it as farce, and robbing it of coherence by dramatizing some of its most important events as discrete, unrelated episodes. By focusing on victimized characters such as Jews from the East End of London, Williams shows that the truth of historical narratives of national self-glorification is not universal but strictly relative to perspective.

Williams fractures the continuous historical narrative by making some of the most famous events of the century disconnected adventures in the chaotic lives of his two central characters, the narrator Amos Barking and his friend Zak Rabinowitz. Amos claims to have "blundered into so many extraordinary encounters, crossed paths with history so many, many times" (59) that his autobiography is virtually a revisionist history of the first half of the twentieth century. In company with an insane and cowardly Field Marshal Douglas Haig, Amos has been shelled in an unrecorded battle of the Great War; at the time of Zak's psychoanalysis with Freud in Vienna, Amos has been employed by the great man's housekeeper to hunt for scandalous information with which to discredit his erstwhile friend Carl Jung; Amos has heard Churchill, in the presence of contemptuous, upper-class friends, make a drunken, vacuous speech in the very rhetorical style that would later make him famous as a war-time prime minister; Amos has beaten a man claiming, in the bizarrely inappropriate accent of New York Jew, to be Joseph Goebbels; and from the air Amos has witnessed the fire bombing of Dresden.

Historiography makes sense of the past after the fact, imputing causes and effects retrospectively, and Amos does look back over his life and times, sometimes from the vantage point of many years. But rather than disclosing patterns of significance, his narration tends to recreate the confused texture of events as he remembers experiencing them at the time. Williams thus reminds us that historical writing might well be oblivious or false to the particular sensations, in all their messiness, of those for whom the history was lived experience. This point is illustrated in Amos's remembrance of being in battle:

> There is no consistency to the images I can recall. The only thing that seems real and true is the mounting sense of fear and horror I felt as we trekked on in the sunshine and, some way ahead, heard the dull thud of guns. . . . I would like to conjure up broken gun-carriages, men with bandaged eyes, shattered lean-tos, an acned, lunar landscape that gave no hope of life ever again. I would like to say I saw the First World War, I suppose. What I saw was an entirely different thing. (96)

This admission is identical to the revelation of Claudia Hampton, the professional historian in Lively's *Moon Tiger*, whose autobiography, like Amos's, is simultaneously a highly selective history, in her case of the entire world. On her death bed she meditates about the relationship between historical accounts of the Allies' campaign during the Second World War against Rommel in the Egyptian desert and her own direct experience there as a correspondent for a newspaper:

> So far as public matters go—history—there is plenty. Most of it is in print now; all those accounts of which general comes out best, who had how many tanks, who advanced where at which point and why. I've read them all; they seem to have little to do with anything I remember. . . . [M]ostly they just don't seem relevant. Which of course is an odd comment from one who has written that kind of book herself. (70)

Recorded histories supply the past with clarity, order, and definition, but novels such as *Moon Tiger* and *Star Turn* question the reality of these patterns of significance. So does Winterson's *The Passion*, in which the narrator Henri, who has been first a cook and then a soldier in Napoleon's army, says of the Emperor: "Nowadays people talk about the things he did as though they made sense. As though even his most disastrous mistakes were only the result of bad luck or hubris. It was a mess" (5).

In order to understand how far-reaching and profound these efforts to make sense may be, and how relevant they are to the study of both historiography and the novel, consider the following catalogue of assumptions which Hillis Miller believes to have been transferred in the eighteenth and nineteenth centuries to the novel from the writing of history:

> They include the notions of origin and end ("archeology" and "teleology"); of unity and totality or "totalization"; of underlying "reason" or "ground": of selfhood, consciousness, or "human nature"; of the homogeneity, linearity,

and continuity of time; of necessary progress; of "fate," "destiny," or "Providence"; of causality; of gradually emerging "meaning" of representation and truth. . . .   (459-60)

Whether or not we assent to Miller's contention (derived from Jacques Derrida) that these ideas are not "diverse attributes" but instead "a true system, in the sense that each implies all the others" (460), we can certainly accept that during the period of which he writes a secular historical consciousness was freighted with values which are broadly religious. Carl Becker argued as long ago as the 1930s that after the scientific revolution the functions of theology were largely taken over by history (17). Much more recently both Byatt (*Passions* 167) and Peter Brooks (6) have stated that the heavily plotted works in the "Great Tradition" of the nineteenth-century novel were substitutes for a providential master-narrative. But, as Byatt says, the crisis of faith which overtook religion has in our own time infected the institution of the novel: "The fictional texts of the Great Tradition are indeed the texts of the Religion of Humanity; and many novelists now seem to feel that they exist in some uneasy relation to the afterlife of these texts, as the texts themselves once coexisted with the afterlife of Genesis and the Gospels. They are the source of enlightenment, but not true. Or not true for us" (*Passions* 167). Becker writes of a corresponding attenuation of the meaning of history: "In the early nineteenth century, history could still be regarded as the Transcendent Idea realizing itself in the actual. In our time history is nothing but history, the notation of what has occurred, just as it happened" (18). That we can no longer confidently share the realist epistemology or the unquestioned belief in the mimetic adequacy of historical writing implied by Becker's last sentence only compounds the dilemma which he diagnoses.

The patterns of narrative significance anatomized above by Miller have not entirely vanished in the novels discussed here but instead stand as glimpsed ideals or dim remembrances in tension with the contingencies and discontinuities that would destroy them. Faith in the grand design of history may have lapsed, but the desire for what has been lost remains. "Coherence and closure are deep human desires that are presently unfashionable," broods *Possession*'s Roland Michell, upon realizing that he and Maud have become participants in the romance plot that drove the actions of Randolph and Christabel. "But they are always both frightening and enchantingly desirable" (422).

This enduring need for meaningful pattern motivates the historical activities of the other novels' protagonists as well. Ackroyd's Charles

Wychwood, for instance, is animated joyfully by his belief that he alone can apprehend in its unity the shape of Thomas Chatterton's life. Wychwood, a poet living in present-day London, has bought a portrait of a figure who appears to be Thomas Chatterton in middle age. Since Chatterton was reputed to have committed suicide at the age of eighteen, Charles infers that the forger of medieval manuscripts did not really die in 1770 but rather lived and wrote on for at least another thirty-two years (the painting is dated 1802). Charles's theory seems to be confirmed when he acquires a manuscript, apparently in Chatterton's hand, in which he claims to have faked suicide and subsequently forged poems attributed to Gray, Akenside, Churchill, Collins, and Blake. In the midst of writing a preface for his planned publication of this document, Charles has a revelation: "All at once he saw the entire pattern of Chatterton's life and with redoubled pressure he wrote it down with his empty pen" (127). After an interruption Charles returns to find his writing faded—"all of his thoughts about Chatterton had disappeared" (128)—and when he tries to replicate those vanished thoughts with a fresh pen, he is at a loss to do more than inscribe the poet's name. The reader learns (although Charles does not) that the historical documents on which he has based his theory about Chatterton's forgeries are fraudulent. Ackroyd is typical in, so to speak, tracing his historical designs with a dry pen (or, perhaps more accurately, with disappearing ink), in denying us "coherence and closure."

Ever After's Bill Unwin has the same disillusioning awareness that his own desire rather than historical fact is behind his reconstruction of the life of his great-great-grandfather, Matthew Pearce, whose notebooks Bill is planning to publish. A widower whose life formerly revolved around his beloved late wife, Ruth, Bill tends to idealize the relationship of Matthew and his wife, Elizabeth. Bill assumes that Elizabeth became the radiant meaning of Matthew's life after his religious faith was destroyed by Darwinian science. But the reality of this pattern of redemption is vitiated when Bill makes the following confession: "That is how I wish it to have happened. I give to Matthew's life that very quality of benign design that he had already glimpsed might be lacking from the universe" (114). He narrates an initial meeting of the couple during which they fall instantly in love, but then he admits that "I invent all this. I don't know that this is how it happened. It can't have been like this simply because I imagine it so" (120). It is but a small step to the more extreme position, voiced here by White, that the ability of narratives to satisfy desires is in itself grounds to dismiss their truth claims: "The notion that sequences of real events possess the formal attributes of the stories we tell about imaginary events could only have its origin in wishes, daydreams, reveries" ("Value of Narrativity" 27).[1]

By means of one formal mechanism or another all of the novels discussed here both stimulate and frustrate the reader's desire for satisfying narrative structures of the sort mentioned by White. It is not *Star Turn* alone of these eight which suggests that the chaos and fluidity of historical processes resist the imposition of neat organizational patterns. As every historian knows, it is impossible to produce an orderly, chronological account of what happened in the order that it happened, for the simple reason that, while writing is necessarily linear, many historically significant events transpire simultaneously. Nevertheless, conventional works of history are, to the extent that it is possible, structured chronologically. In being unconventionally organized, Lively's *Moon Tiger* claims to respond more honestly to the perception of its historian-protagonist, Claudia, that "[h]istory is disorder" (152).

The narrative pattern of *Moon Tiger* is a response not only to this disorder but also to the way in which the historian writing the history experiences time. Events, however chaotic and elusive of understanding, occur in time, but, as David Daiches many years ago astutely observed, "the relation of consciousness to time is not the simple one of events to time, but is independent of chronological sequence in a way that events are not" (16). Early in the novel, Claudia makes a virtually identical point: "Chronology irritates me. There is no chronology inside my head. . . . The pack of cards I carry around is forever shuffled and reshuffled; there is no sequence, everything happens at once" (2). As a consequence, the model or analogy for the structure of her contemplated history of the world (which is, of course, Lively's already completed, highly self-conscious novel) is the kaleidoscope: "Shake the tube and see what comes out" (2). The image of the kaleidoscope suggests the transformation of time into a spatial pattern of the sort that Joseph Frank associated with the modernist novel. *Moon Tiger* is also redolent of the modernist novel in featuring a stream-of-consciousness narrative technique. Much like *Mrs. Dalloway* (though not in Woolf's highly lyrical style), Lively's narrative moves supply around in time, sometimes unpredictably, as Claudia's memories of people and experiences dictate.

---

[1] As David Perkins notes, this conclusion rests on a fallacy: "[t]hat our historical narratives gratify desires does not prove that they are misrepresentations, for the emotional satisfactions we get from a story have no relation to the criteria by which we estimate its truth" (*Is Literary History Possible?* 35).

Whereas the fugitive reminiscences and sensations of Woolf's characters usually take the form of poetic reveries, Claudia's remembrances are more typically subsumed within, or related to, her meditations on historical subjects which have interested her professionally.[2]

Is it just the mind's experience of time alone—the *durée* of Henri Bergson—which resists chronological sequence, or is it time itself (and human interactions in time) which gives the lie to the mechanically regular patterning of clocks and calendars? Is it true, as R. G. Collingwood holds, that "there is only one historical world, and [that] everything in it must stand in some relation to everything else, even if that relation is only topographical and chronological" (246)? This assertion that human events stand in a stable, determinate chronological relation to one another flies in the face of Claudia's musings in *Moon Tiger* about Egypt and its history: "I cannot write chronologically of Egypt. . . . I have to think of it as a continuous phenomenon, the kilted pharaonic population spilling out into the Nile valley of the twentieth century. . . . Past and present do not so much co-exist in the Nile valley as cease to have any meaning" (80). This characterization of Egypt is identical to the way one of *The Passion*'s narrators, Villanelle, thinks of her home, Venice, and its gondoliers: "There is a certainty that comes with the oars, with the sense of generation after generation standing up like this and rowing like this with rhythm and ease. This city is littered with ghosts seeing to their own. . . . All time is eternally present and so all time is ours" (61-62). The separate points in time collapse, not only because of the vagaries of Claudia's and Villanelle's memories, but, presumably, also because time is in some basic sense an unstable phenomenon. For Claudia its malleability seems to issue from nature itself, which is not characterized by temporal progression but by cyclical recurrence; she speaks of the "eternal, deliberate cycle of the landscape—the sun rising from the desert of

---

[2] The comparison of Lively to Woolf raises the possibility that their common sex might underlie the formal innovations which I have been discussing, and Mary Hurley Moran does argue that Claudia's ideas about time and her unorthodox approach to the writing of history reveal "a subversive feminist outlook" (90). It would be a mistake, however, to overemphasize the importance of feminism in Claudia's professional life, since she declines to associate her achievements with this movement. "My gender was never an impediment," she says. "And I must also reflect now, that it perhaps saved my life. If I had been a man I might well have died in the war" (14). Moreover, her interest in the "great men" of history (she has published books on Cortez and Tito) places her squarely in the patriarchal tradition of orthodox historiography, not the more recent practice of social history, which focuses on the lives of women and other formerly excluded groups.

the east to sink into the desert of the west, the spring surge of the river, the regeneration of creatures . . . , the enduring peasantry" (80-81).

The structure of *Chatterton* also challenges the notion that time provides a secure framework for human history. The novel has three subplots set in what seem to be distinctly separate eras: the late twentieth century of Charles Wychwood, Harriet Scrope, and the other modern characters; the late eighteenth century of Thomas Chatterton; and the mid-nineteenth century of both Henry Wallis, who painted the famous portrait of Chatterton on his death bed, and the poet George Meredith, who served as the model for the painting. In certain parts of the novel, however, the pace with which the subplots succeed one another accelerates, and there are junctures at which these ostensibly parallel time-lines intersect. At the point of death, Chatterton has a complex vision in which he is both perpetually passing one young man, who shows him a puppet, on an old stone staircase, and is also perpetually standing near a fountain behind another young man who bows his head in pain (233). Readers know, although Chatterton does not, that the first young man is George Meredith, who reports having dreamed encountering Chatterton in exactly the situation that Chatterton sees (139), and that the second young man is Charles Wychwood, who, in the throes of a seizure, has briefly seen a mysterious young man near a fountain (47). Chatterton also appears before Charles in the Kubla Khan Restaurant just at the moment when he collapses as a result of the brain tumour that will take his life (152), and, as if to confirm that this vision cannot be explained away as a private hallucination, Harriet Scrope, who is dining with Charles and a few others, also, quite independently, sees Chatterton (166).

Chatterton suggests, then, that the past is never really past, since it can merge with the present, which in turn can be visited by the future. As Brian Finney states, "Ackroyd's vision is essentially atemporal" (257). Historical events that seem to be sequential and completed may be, in some mysterious sense, synchronous and unfinished. If this is so, should we change the way in which we conceive of events? Do events, in their slipperiness, exist in an empirical, objective sense as discrete phenomena? Louis Mink's answer to this question is thought-provoking:

[H]ardly any concept is less clear than that of "event." . . . Uncertainty sets in when we consider the limits of application of the concept. Are there simple or unit-events, that is, events which are not further divisible into events? At the other extreme, what is the maximum complexity and time span beyond which the application of the term is inappropriate? . . . Moreover, it is clear that we cannot refer to events as such, but only to events *under a description*; so there can be more than one description of the same event, all of them true but referring to different aspects of the event or describing it at different levels of generality. But what can we possibly mean by "same event"?

(199-200)

Even more problematic are contradictory descriptions of the "same event." Must one be objectively false and the other objectively true, or are the answers to such questions strictly relative to the premises and interpretive schemes of the claimants? "'Events,'" Mink concludes, "are not the raw material out of which narratives are constructed; rather, an event is an abstraction from a narrative" (201). And what is it that validates the truth-claims of historical narratives? Without denying that there are matters of fact which historiography cannot ignore, Mink dispenses with "the idea that there is a determinate historical actuality, the complex referent for all our stories of 'what actually happened,' the untold story to which narrative histories approximate" (202).

Fowles's *A Maggot* could be read as confirming Mink's views about the relationship between events and narrative. The novel contests the positivist assumption that there is a single, verifiable reality underlying historical representations. The work is structured so as to highlight the necessarily retrospective, distanced nature of historical reconstruction, to emphasize the unbridgeable gulf between a supposedly objective event and descriptions of it. The first fifty-two pages, in conventional novelistic form, immerse readers in the narrative present of an eighteenth-century journey from London to Devonshire undertaken by an unnamed young aristocrat, whose pseudonym is Mr. Bartholomew, and four underlings, whom he has recruited. This section breaks off before the final destination has been reached, and the bulk of the novel takes the form of the transcript of an inquiry conducted by the barrister Henry Ayscough several months after the completion of the journey and the mysterious disappearance of Bartholomew, whose father has employed the barrister to locate his son. *A Maggot* thus directs attention to history not only because it is set in the eighteenth century but also because one strand of its plot consists of an attempt to reconstruct the past. According to testimony elicited by Ayscough, the young lord failed to reemerge from a cavern, in which took place, apparently, an enigmatic series of events, involving the prostitute Rebecca Lee, one of Bartholomew's party, and three other unidentified female figures, who have also disappeared without a trace.

What happened in the cavern, and what caused Bartholomew to vanish, and his servant, the deaf-mute Dick Thurlow, to hang himself?

These are the enigmas which the arch-empiricist Ayscough intends to clear up, but the only available reports of the extraordinary affair are supplied by Rebecca Lee, the lone eyewitness. She is in the position of Forster's Adela Quested, but the ambiguity about what happened in *A Passage to India*'s famous Marabar cave is mild compared to the radical uncertainty created by Rebecca's unreliable testimony. The reader is free to interpret what she says as evidence of an intent to deceive, a hallucination, a mystical vision, or an encounter with extra-terrestrials. What breeds doubt about her credibility is not only the fantastic character of her tale of ascending to a heavenly city in a flying saucer or "maggot" but also the fact that she had earlier told David Jones (another of Bartholomew's travelling companions) a completely different, contradictory version of the story, in which she had unwillingly participated in an orgiastic, infernal rite. In this first version, Bartholomew disappeared because he was claimed by Satan (260); in the second, the aristocrat, now embodying the spirit of Christ, remained in the celestial "June Eternal" while Rebecca returned to earth in the maggot (381). Although she repudiates the tale which she had told Jones (300), her sworn testimony does not cancel or replace the first account in the reader's consciousness but stands next to it. One version is no more credible than the other. The effect of this duality is to place *A Maggot* in the category of what Seymour Chatman calls "antinarratives" because "what they call into question is, precisely, narrative logic, that one thing leads to one and only one other, the second to a third and so on to the finale" (57).

Ayscough, like the protagonist of standard detective fiction (Essex 81; Edgar 29-30), tries to discover the objective truth that he believes lies beyond Lee's two narrative accounts of what happened to Bartholomew. In the terms of Russian formalism, this actuality corresponds to the *fabula* or story, "the sum total of events to be related in the narrative," whereas Lee's tales correspond to two versions of the *sjuzet* or plot, "the story as actually told by linking events together" (Chatman 19-20). But despite Ayscough's best efforts, in *A Maggot* the *fabula*—Mink's "determinate historical actuality"—is nowhere to be found. Tzvetan Todorov says that "the story is what has happened in life, the plot is the way that the author presents it to us" (45), but Fowles's message seems to be that various narrative plots may be our only guide to what actually happened "in life" in the past. As Peter Brooks notes, the *fabula* "is in fact a mental construction that the reader derives from the *sjuzet*, which is all that he ever directly knows" (13). But as Todorov has shown, detective fiction has traditionally created a powerful illusion of the independent reality of the *fabula*, the crime which has been committed and which must be reconstructed by the detective in the *sjuzet* in order to be resolved. Todorov argues that the second order of story, the detective's inquest, "has no importance in itself" but "serves only as a mediator between the reader and the story of the crime" (46). Fowles destroys this hierarchy, however, because the "crime" cannot be reconstructed empirically. It is impossible to infer a coherent *fabula* from what Rebecca says, since her two accounts are not reconcilable on a literal level.

Interestingly enough, they are compatible on a symbolic level, if read as opposite but integral stages of a unified psychological process of development which both Rebecca and Bartholomew may have undergone. Adopting a Jungian viewpoint, Walter Miller, Jr. makes this point in noticing that each of Rebecca's versions features a "numinous female triad linked to a mysterious fourth—three witches and Satan (the lord transformed), or a female Holy Trinity joined by a harlot." Miller concludes that the "equivalence of the infernal and celestial versions of the scene in the cave conforms to Jung's psychology, and both versions of the cave scene are true" (11). Perhaps what Fowles wants readers to see is that such symbolic patterns of significance may be more important than literal historical truth of the sort that Ayscough demands and fails to attain.

In writing about the elastic, non-linear qualities of time, the chaotic nature of historical processes, the ambiguous character of events, and their relationship to the narrative representations on which our knowledge of those events depends, I have been focusing on those formal or structural aspects of the novels which suggest not only the vexed character of our knowledge of the past but also our freedom from the apparent constraints of history. If events are not final, if we are not locked into a single irrevocable sequence, if there are many historical worlds, not just the one world which Collingwood mentions in the quotation above, then history is not the coercive force which it appears to be. But one should neither over-emphasize the plasticity of time nor obscure the severe limitations which, the novels imply, history does in fact impose on us. Chief among these limitations is individual mortality. Lively's Claudia, for example, may meditate on the illusory quality of time, but the fact that hers is a death-bed narrative reminds us that her life span is finite. Speculate though she will upon the historical continuities that blur the distinction between past and present, she herself has been separated by death from Tom Southern, the young man killed in the Egyptian campaign who had been her lover. After reading his diary for

31

the first time, many years after his death, Claudia remarks on the painful, uncrossable abyss which history has dug between them:

> We are no longer in the same story, and when I read what you wrote I think of all that you do not know. You are left behind, in another place and another time, and I am someone else, not the C. of whom you thought, . . . but an unimaginable Claudia from whom you would recoil, perhaps. A stranger, inhabiting a world you would not recognize. I find this hard to bear. (206)

Chatterton also at times registers the implacable, unitary drive of historical forces. The novel may feature a few mysterious occurrences, perhaps of a spiritual nature, which are free from the restrictions of chronology, and, as I have said, the book does appear to question the finality of physical death. But is this tantamount to a denial of death's power? On the contrary, *Chatterton* could be said to be obsessively concerned with death. The untimely, tragic suicide of the "marvellous boy" is what, along with his forgeries, Chatterton is famous for, and the demise of his modern counterpart, the poet Charles Wychwood, is so heavily foreshadowed throughout that it comes to seem as fated and inevitable as that of Chatterton himself. Charles's death certainly seems real and permanent to his devastated little son, Edward, and to his wife, Vivien. The nineteenth-century subplot is also focused on death, revolving as it does around Meredith's impersonation of Chatterton's corpse as the model for Wallis's portrait.

Depending on the particular narratives in question, organizational patterns which feature chronological dislocations can be seen not so much to deny as to confirm the linear sweep of history. The mind of *Ever After*'s narrator Bill Unwin meanders and circles over emotionally charged events which happened in many different stages of his life, but he does not make time over into an aesthetically pleasing shape, such as the kaleidoscopic array of Claudia Hampton. The violations of a linear temporal sequence do not so much suggest the metamorphosis of time into space as a neurotic obsession with particular, disturbing moments in time that Bill is compelled to play over and over again in his mind. Much as *Waterland*'s Tom Crick obsessively returns to his father's discovery of Freddie Parr's drowned body and to other traumatic occurrences, Bill repeatedly adverts to his father's suicide. The question of what motivated his father haunts him. So does the possibility that Ruth (who, dying of lung cancer, also committed suicide) was secretly adulterous, as his mother had been. The novel concludes, though, not with an unhappy event from Bill's past, nor where the story began, in the emotional desert of Bill's narrative present (in which he sorrowfully convalesces after a failed suicide attempt), but rather with his reminiscence of the glorious night many years before during which he and Ruth were sexually intimate for the first time. He thus makes the consummation of their love the radiant meaning towards which the entire narrative has moved teleologically.

In affirming the power of the mind to order his life story as desire dictates, Swift's gloomy protagonist is trying, after all, to rob time of its victory by tapping a source of joy and meaning which he had experienced in the past. Swift seems to want the novel's ending to have a transforming function similar to that discussed by Frank Kermode in relation to the Christian Apocalypse: "the End changes all, and produces, in what in relation to it is the past, these seasons, *kairoi*, historical moments of intemporal significance. The divine plot is the pattern of *kairoi* in relation to the End" (47). Bill's ending, of course, is meant to restore his lost wife, but he also wants it to transform his father's suicide, the news of which he discloses to Ruth on the magical night in question. The last two sentences of the novel read as follows: "How impossible that either of these young people, whose lives, this night, have never been so richly possessed, so richly embraced, will ever come to such a pass. He took his life, he took his life" (276). As Lorna Sage notes, what is being attempted here is "to redeem a sterile, suicidal statement ('He took his own life') by turning it round into a creative act, a celebration of people's irreplaceableness: tragedy, not postmodern farce" (6). Bathed in the romantic glow of his love for Ruth, the nihilism of his father's suicide becomes a positive act, a seizing of life.

What undermines the novel's conclusion is precisely our knowledge that what it narrates is part of the ongoing flux, not the terminus of a purposeful design larger than that which Swift himself has fashioned in *Ever After*. A divine plot is just what Bill, like his Victorian ancestor Matthew before him, has been unable to persuade himself to believe in. Since we know that Ruth also eventually did "come to such a pass" as a suicide, we cannot help but see irony in the novel's final statement, despite the lyrical passion and tenderness which infuse it. Their wonderful night together was not the end of history but rather a transient experience, however centrally important it was to both. That experience could not alter or terminate the course of history, a fact which the shape of the narrative paradoxically underscores. Making Bill's reminiscence of that special night the novel's denouement has the ironical effect of heightening his loss. Bill's imaginative reconstruction provides solace, to be sure, but it is double-edged in painfully reminding him and us of what time and death have taken away from him.

33

CHAPTER TWO

Textual Fragmentation and the Proliferation of Genres: History as Dialogic

It is not Swift's novel alone that fosters suspicion of narrative patterns which satisfy the longing for wholeness and purpose. This need is frustrated by a structural feature prominent in numerous contemporary novels: textual fragmentation or deformation of a kind that makes more difficult the totalization—the all-encompassing, unified understanding—associated by Hillis Miller in a previously quoted passage with both the novel and the writing of history. It is fairly typical for postmodernist novels to present themselves as unintegrated agglomerations of different kinds of documents. *A Maggot* and *Possession,* for example, both incorporate several kinds of writing in a variety of styles. Into the sections of *Possession* written in the traditional form of the realistic novel (employing third-person narration and Jamesian centres of consciousness) Byatt has inserted poems, fairy tales, personal letters, excerpts from diaries, biographies, and works of literary criticism. *A Maggot* also features both segments of narrative in the manner of a realistic novel and other kinds of documents, some of which Fowles has taken from authentic eighteenth-century sources and some of which he has composed to masquerade as eighteenth-century texts. In the former category are excerpts from the "Historical Chronicle" for 1736 of the *Gentleman's Magazine* and a misogynist satire, culled from the same periodical, titled "Pretty Miss's Catechism." In the latter category are a newspaper account of Dick Thurlow's death, personal letters, and hundreds of pages of transcripts in question-and-answer format of testimony which Ayscough elicits during his inquiry. What the juxtaposition of discourses highlights in both books is the textuality of history, the constructedness of any account in language of the way things are. In the proximity of other kinds of writing with markedly different conventions, the passages in the form of realistic fiction no longer seem to be transparent windows disclosing an objective reality.

Ever After does not manifest textual splintering to the same degree as do the works by Fowles and Byatt, but nevertheless the novel cannot comfortably hold together all of the diverse experiences and points of time which it would contain. Bill's aim is to fashion a single, didactic narrative which makes sense of his own life in the larger context of nineteenth- and twentieth-century history. He views the Victorian story as an integral aspect of that overall narrative. For Matthew's tragic, perhaps stupidly obstinate, decision to publicly avow his crisis of religious faith—even at the cost of his marriage—can be read as a contrast illustrating the rightness of Bill's own total commitment to Ruth and his marriage to her as the most important value in life. Moreover, he sees the nineteenth-century story as supplying the resolution of the dilemma which he faces in the narrative present: the failure of the love between him and Ruth to sustain him after her death. What I mean is that the reanimation or resurrection of Matthew through the narrative that Bill creates from the journal is intended to be his consolation for the loss of Ruth. Adding to the effect of cohesive design is that, while the novel contains entries from Matthew's notebooks and a letter to Elizabeth, all in a pastiche of Victorian style, *Ever After* is dominated by Bill's much less formal writing, with its distinctive texture and rhythms. Swift employs a certain amount of dialogue and dramatization, but Bill is essentially a monologist, given to Hamlet-like soliloquizing, who has tried to assimilate a fragmentary outer reality into a more unified interior one.

The pressures working against such totalization strain almost to the breaking point Bill's efforts to achieve narrative smoothness and unity. Bill is anxiously aware that other voices should counter and supplement his own, but he also knows that beyond the faint traces which they have left in the historical record, the dead cannot speak. His epistemological difficulties in trying to assume other points of view breed a self-conscious, questioning style and tone which, as Sage notices, expresses "the ambition to hold things together, but sketchily, as though they are also always falling apart" (6). At one point, as if to acknowledge the inadequacy of his chosen narrative form, Bill briefly experiments with another—the television script—in trying to dramatize the confrontation between the atheist Matthew and his clergyman father-in-law. This proves even less satisfactory, however, and Bill breaks off, after a failed attempt to imagine the rector's angry response to his son-in-law, with the following remark: "But I do not know, I cannot even invent, what the Rector said. I falter in my script-writing, just as the Rector himself, perhaps, faltered on the verge of his imprecation" (199).

The most extreme example of textual hybridism from the works I have selected is *A History of the World in 10 1/2 Chapters*, which more closely resembles a collection of diverse (albeit thematically related) short fictions than the novel which the book's dust jacket promises. Written from many different perspectives in a variety of stylistic registers and cast in incommensurable modes of writing, Barnes's work crosses ontological boundaries while refusing to construct a stabilizing hierarchy of meanings. No single discourse achieves authority, not a convincing pastiche of an actual historical account from the early nineteenth century of the wreck of the ship *Medusa*, not the transcript of a legal proceeding, nor even Scripture, which is parodied in the form of a revisionist retelling, from the point of view of a stowaway termite, of the story in Genesis of Noah and the Ark.

Nor is any special privilege achieved by the section of Barnes's book which seems to be written most directly from his own point of view as author: the disquisition on love in "Parenthesis," in which he "fret[s] at the obliquities of fiction" (225) and seems to invite us to accept his meditation as a heartfelt personal philosophy. As Donald Pease states, "the term 'author' raises questions about authority and whether the individual is the source or effect of that authority. The word 'author' derives from the medieval term *auctor*, which denoted a writer whose words commanded respect and belief" (106). Pease goes on to explain that the individual genius of the modern author came to replace the cultural tradition of the medieval *auctor* as the sanction for the views of a literary work (108-11). Readers might be tempted to grant special authority to Barnes's ideas on love on the basis of his creativity. Personal sincerity and deep feeling seem to ground his eloquent defense of love, but the very fact that his are avowedly personal views raises the spectre of their subjectivity. "That's my theory, anyway" (241), says the narrator, defensively (with reference to his liberal approach to the sexual indiscretions of politicians), thereby reminding us of the existence of competing, equally plausible theories.

Some of Barnes's other discourses strive to be authoritative in different ways, but each is undercut by virtue of the overall context in which he places them: a postmodernist one in which foundational or master narratives do not exist. Take, for example, the historical account in "Shipwreck" of the ordeal suffered by the French seamen and passengers cast adrift on a raft after the frigate *Medusa* struck a reef in July 1816. Barnes tells us in the "Author's Note" that for this part of "Shipwreck" he drew "its facts and language from the 1818 London translation of Savigny and Corréard's *Narrative of a Voyage to Senegal*" (308). Resting on the first-hand knowledge of the authors, who survived the disaster, this nineteenth-century source text seems to have considerable authenticity. The rhetoric which Barnes employs here is confident, emotionally poised, even magisterial; as the following passage attests, the perspective is seemingly one that the authors, as participants, could not have had: that of a god who can look down on the plight of the sailors and describe it with perfect equanimity, objectivity, and precision:

> The raft, which now carried less than one half of its original complement, had risen up in the water, an unforeseen benefit of the night's mutinies. Yet those on board remained in water to the knees, and could only repose standing up, pressed against one another in a solid mass. On the fourth morning they perceived that a dozen of their fellows had died in the night; their bodies were given to the sea, except for one that was reserved against their hunger. At four o'clock that afternoon a shoal of flying fish passed over the raft, and many became ensnared in the extremities of the machine. That night they dressed the fish, but their hunger was so great and each portion so exiguous, that many of them added human flesh to the fish, and the flesh being dressed was found less repugnant. Even the officers began to eat it when presented in this form. (120)

This is the sort of historical writing which, according to White, does not so much narrate as "narrativize." He coins this term in the process of distinguishing "between a [narrated] discourse that openly adopts a perspective that looks out on the world and reports it and a [narrativized] discourse that feigns to make the world speak itself and speak itself *as a story*" ("Value of Narrativity" 6-7). In other words, writing of the kind quoted above serenely implies that it constitutes the complete, objective truth, not a situated, fallible representation of the affair.

What undermines the authority of the historical narrative in the first part of "Shipwreck" is nothing intrinsic to it but rather the second part, which deals, in a markedly more self-conscious style, with Theodore Géricault's famous painting of the raft. In sensitizing us to the political context of the *Medusa* disaster (the conflict between Bonapartists and monarchists), the second part makes us realize that the narrative in the first part did not adequately reflect the monarchist perspective on the shipwreck. We see that the apparently definitive, complete account provided in the first part is an illusion created by rhetoric rather than a result of authentically godlike knowledge. Could any single version encompass all of the possibly relevant considerations? Could any satisfy the changing expectations and values which successive generations of readers might impose on such a narrative? Clearly, Barnes does not think so:

> Nowadays, as we examine [Géricault's] "Scene of a Shipwreck," it is hard to feel much indignation against Hughes Duroy de Chaumareys, captain of the

expedition, or against the minister who appointed him captain, or the naval officer who refused to skipper the raft, or the soldiery who mutinied. (Indeed, history democratizes our sympathies. Had not the soldiers been brutalized by their wartime experiences? Was not the captain a victim of his own pampered upbringing? Would we bet on ourselves to behave heroically in similar circumstances?) (133)

Another type of writing which Barnes incorporates into the book is that of the legal transcript, which would seem by its very nature to command authority. The law has behind it the official imprimatur and power of the state. But such authority is not timeless, as Barnes reminds us by fabricating the transcript of an early sixteenth-century proceeding (based, he claims in the "Author's Note," on a real case [308]) in France against woodworms which had infested a church and caused a bishop to be seriously injured when the damaged chair in which he sat collapsed. By our modern standards, it is self-evidently absurd to try non-humans for breaking human laws, the existence of which they could not possibly comprehend. The advocate defending the woodworms does, in fact, make this point (65-66), but, because of the central position of the church in such a theocracy, in order to have a chance to plead his case successfully he needs to square his argument with Christian theology, as does the prosecutor as well. All parties (with the exception of the woodworms, of course) accept Scripture as a master narrative, something which the reader constructed by Barnes cannot do. For the satirical first chapter of Barnes's *History of the World* totally discredits the account in Genesis of Noah's voyage, on which the arguments of both lawyers rest. And, in any event, "The Wars of Religion" reminds us that even in sixteenth-century France, the Bible did not speak its own meanings. They were then and are now the product of interpretations, and the bloody battles between Catholics and Huguenots (to which the title of Barnes's story refers) showed how disturbingly irreconcilable competing interpretations may be.

Textual heterogeneity of the sort which I have been discussing has two somewhat contradictory sets of implications, depending upon whether we apply a deconstructionist logic or a Bakhtinian one. It would be possible to emphasize the inevitably fabricated nature of all historical representations—in other words, the baselessness of a world in which there is nothing outside the text—or, more hopefully, the opportunities for personal and political change given by a situation in which at all levels the meanings of language, however unstable, however unconnected to a "transcendental signified," are generated by the interactions of individuals and groups in society. As Eagleton states, "though lan-

guage may not be best understood as individual expression, '
in some ways involves human subjects and their intentions, ؛
which the structuralist picture leaves out of account" (*Literary*
113). Waugh amplifies on the respects in which Bakhtin's work, with ɪ؛
emphasis on human agency, anticipated postmodernism: "Bakhtin's
dialogism sees knowledge of the world, self and other, as always historically situated, relational, open-ended and perspectival, a process shifting through time and space. None of these categories is a self-sufficient
construct, but a relational process anchored in provisional and continuous 'authorships'" (*Practising Postmodernism* 59).

As LaCapra points out, the practice of historiography is essentially
dialogic or polyphonic in character, "in that, through it, the historian
enters into a 'conversational' exchange with the past and with other
inquirers seeking an understanding of it" (36). This dialogical character
tends to be effaced in conventional historical writing, at least to the
extent that the historian adopts an authoritative, "monological" voice
which assimilates, or at least subordinates, the other voices. But the
historian may counteract this impression both from without—by giving
more prominence to the other voices that are part of the "conversation"
—and from within, as LaCapra explains, following Bakhtin: "the voice of
the historian may be internally 'dialogized' when it undergoes the
appeal of different interpretations, employs self-critical reflection about
its own protocols of inquiry, and makes use of modes such as irony,
parody, self-parody, and humor, that is, double- or multiple-voiced uses
of language" (36).

Lively's Claudia deliberately makes her unorthodox history of the
world dialogic in the senses which LaCapra suggests. As we have already
seen, she incorporates a level of meta-discourse, which self-consciously
interrogates her own procedures as a historian. Her views on language
certainly echo Bakhtin's emphasis on the social and historical rather
than private and individual nature of discourse (Bakhtin 259). "In a
single sentence of idle chatter," says Claudia, "we preserve Latin, Anglo-
Saxon, Norse; we carry a museum inside our heads, each day we commemorate peoples of whom we have never even heard" (41). Claudia's
acceptance of relativism also accords with Bakhtin's thinking. Although
arrogantly self-assured and overbearing, she nevertheless makes no
special claims for the objective truth of her historical representations.
"Beliefs are relative," she says. "Our connection with reality is always
tenuous" (8). Consequently, she repudiates the single, detached, authoritative narrative voice of orthodox histories: "I shall use many voices
in this history. Not for me the cool level tone of dispassionate narration"

39

(8). Believing, as she does, that history is "a babble of voices" (15), she decides to give a hearing to those individuals who have played significant roles in her life: "[m]y story is tangled with the stories of others—Mother, Gordon, Jasper, Lisa, and one other person above all; their voices must be heard also" (5-6).

The method by which Lively actualizes Claudia's intentions in *Moon Tiger* is to use multiple perspectives in narrating the book's episodes. Claudia's voice is countered by that of an undramatized narrator and also by the voices of other characters. She often dramatizes the "same" event more than once, showing how radically different it can seem to different individuals, even members of the same family. For example, as Claudia, her fatally ill brother, Gordon, and his wife, Sylvia, ride together in a taxi, Claudia and Gordon argue passionately, as they have done since they were children. The scene is dramatized first from Sylvia's perspective: "'Rubbish!' says Claudia. 'Absolute rubbish!' And Sylvia jumps, staunches the flow of thought, turns to the here and now. . . . How *can* Claudia! Coming back at him like that when he's so ill. Interrupting. Raising her voice. Typical Claudia. It's appalling. When he's . . . when he's going to die" (185). The scene is immediately replayed from Claudia's point of view in a way that lets the reader see that Sylvia (who knows nothing of the incest which Gordon and Claudia indulged in as adolescents) misunderstands what the argument signifies emotionally for her husband and his sister:

> "Rubbish!" says Claudia. It sounds vehement enough; it sounds almost as though she means it. Her eyes meet Gordon's, and she sees that he is not fooled, but he goes on talking and she goes on talking and interrupting and beneath what is said they tell each other something entirely different.
>
> I love you, she thinks. Always have. More than I've loved anyone, bar one. (185)

The shifts in perspective often undercut rather than support Claudia's perceptions and opinions. For example, inside views of Lisa, Claudia's daughter, show how flawed and partial Claudia's dismissive perceptions of her are. In Claudia's eyes, Lisa is disappointingly timid, conventional, and untalented, but the reader learns that her daughter has greater abilities and a much richer life than Claudia suspects. The reader also learns that, ironically, Claudia herself has unintentionally moulded the side of Lisa that Claudia disparages:

> Lisa is extinguished by Claudia, always has been; even now . . . she sits warily, awaiting Claudia's next move. Claudia snuffs Lisa out—drains the colour from her cheeks, deprives her of . . . all speech to which anyone might pay

attention, makes her shrink an inch or two, puts her in her place. The other Lisa, the Lisa unknown to Claudia, is positive while not assertive, is prettier, sharper, a good cook, a competent mother, an adequate if not exemplary wife. (60)

As my analysis of its textual fragmentation has already demonstrated without using Bakhtin's terminology, Barnes's *History* is also dialogic in the senses which LaCapra describes above. Although Barnes seems to speak directly in certain places, he must compete for space with many other speakers with quite distinct perspectives and styles. Some of these characters narrate their own stories, such as the desperate female protagonist of "The Survivor" and the woodworm who has stowed away on Noah's Ark in Chapter One. No authorial mediation is detectable in these stories, or in "Upstream!" which consists entirely of personal letters written in colourful, demotic prose to his girlfriend in England by an actor making a movie in South America. In these chapters, as I've already intimated, Barnes makes considerable use of irony, parody, and other forms of doubly-oriented discourse. "Upstream!" for example, falls into the category of comic fiction mentioned by Bakhtin which features "parodic stylizations of generic, professional and other languages" (302). The actor's extravagant, egocentric letters reveal bohemian attitudes, a roistering lifestyle, and views on acting which parody a recognizable stereotype: that of the actor as the larger-than-life, passionate, existential hero. As we have already seen, Barnes's *History of the World* also contains meta-discourse that self-consciously interrogates its own procedures.

What this dialogic flux permits in Barnes's *History of the World* and in some of the other fictional texts under consideration is a contesting or even rewriting of standard or orthodox accounts of, or ways of thinking about, the past. I have already discussed *Star Turn*'s treatment of the first fifty years of the twentieth century in this light. In Barnes's "Stowaway," the insubordinate, irreverent voice of the woodworm counteracts the dogmatic, patriarchal voices of Noah and the Old Testament God. Jeanette Winterson's *The Passion* is another example of what McHale calls "the postmodernist revisionist historical novel" (90). The book's ironic treatment of Napoleon and the myth of heroic national destiny which he embodies debunks the "Great Men" model of history. Winterson's version of Napoleon's ill-fated invasion of Russia is told from the perspectives of historically insignificant figures, who are the victims and losers of war. One of the two narrators, the French peasant Henri, identifies with Napoleon and his imperialistic ideal, but in his diary he is nevertheless unable to echo the Emperor's monologic voice of absolute authority. "He believed he was the centre of the world and for a long time there was nothing to change him from this belief" (13), says Henri of Napoleon, and it is this certainty that Henri hopes to share in his blind hero-worship of his leader. The only certainty which he attains, though, comes out of his suffering and loss of humanity as a victim of Napoleon's Russian campaign: "Now that our hearts were gone there was no reliable organ to stem the steady tide of sentiment that stuck to our bayonets and fed our damp fires. There was nothing we wouldn't believe to get us through: God was on our side, the Russians were devils. Our wives depended on this war. France depended on this war. There was no alternative to this war" (83). This bogus assurance fades as the nationalistic ideal on which it depends is shattered by the defeat suffered by the French forces.

In any event, Henri's journal is characterized not by such black-and-white certitude but by diffidence and a self-conscious questioning of the validity of his own historical record. He writes of the difficulty of "trying to convey to you what really happened. Trying not too make up too much" (103). LaCapra's terms are, perhaps, inappropriately grandiose to apply to the uneducated Henri, but it could nevertheless be said that his words constitute "self-critical reflection about [his] own protocols of inquiry" (36).

Those protocols include attempts, such as the following, to record events empirically with objective accuracy: "July 20, 1804. Two thousand men were drowned today" (24). Much more typical, however, are equally stark but more poetic utterances which convey Henri's subjective impressions and feelings, not objective facts. This aim is expressed overtly in one of the book's self-reflexive moments, as Henri responds to his compatriot Domino, who criticizes his decision to keep a written record:

> "What makes you think you can see anything clearly? What gives you the right to make a notebook and shake it at me in thirty years, if we're still alive, and say you've got the truth?"
> "I don't care about the facts, Domino, I care about how I feel. How I feel will change, I want to remember that." (28-29)

For both Henri and the second narrator, the androgynous Villanelle, a language of feeling replaces the dispassionate style and rational organization of orthodox historical writing. It is possible that Winterson sees the monologic accounts of traditional historiography—in which events are mapped out in a progressive, linear order—as flawed by the same imperious, patriarchal conception of things that Napoleon would impose by force on Europe. The dialogically counterpointed narrations of Henri and Villanelle instead correspond, in their more fluid, meandering paths, to Villanelle's home of Venice, as Henri describes it: "Where Bonaparte goes, straight roads follow, buildings are rationalised, street signs may change to celebrate a battle but they are always clearly marked. Here, if they bother with street signs at all, they are happy to use the same ones over again. Not even Bonaparte could rationalise Venice" (112).

The dialogism of *A Maggot* also serves one kind of feminist resistance to patriarchal authority, in this case embodied by the barrister Ayscough and the ruling aristocrats who employ him. We have already seen that his attempt to construct a definitive, objective account of what happened to Bartholomew is stymied by Rebecca Lee's refusal to adopt his perspective on things. The open-endedness and ambiguity of the novel is a consequence of her recalcitrance. Ayscough is rational, empirical, legalistic, authoritarian, conservative and misogynistic, whereas Lee is intuitive, imaginative, artistic, visionary, democratic, and revolutionary. Ayscough is obviously meant to be seen as a representative male of the early eighteenth-century, a champion of reason and neo-classical tradition. In contrast, Lee, as the novel's epilogue makes clear, anticipates romantic individualism and reliance on feeling (451).

It is not merely the opposition of Lee and her dissenting religious sect to the established order which prevents the discourse of aristocracy from prevailing in monologic fashion. A challenge to its dominance is mounted by the mere existence of what Bakhtin calls "heteroglossia *within* a language," by which he means "internal differentiation, the stratification characteristic of any national language" (67). *A Maggot* presents us with the regional dialects of Devon and Wales; the writing and speaking styles of the aristocracy; the deferential speech patterns of those who serve them; the languages of legal system, stage, and brothel; the specialized, tendentious vocabulary of religious dissent; and even the modern argot of a twentieth-century narrator, who is trying to understand and explain the eighteenth-century world his characters take for granted.

This polyphony supports the novel's obvious thematic bias in favour of the egalitarian political subtext of religious dissent. (The sect with which Lee is associated is a forerunner of the Shakers, founded by the real historical figure Ann Lee, whom Fowles imagines to be the daughter of his entirely fictional character Rebecca.) The bias does not destroy the book's dialogism because Fowles refuses to make the tyrannical

Ayscough a straw man. He has a formidable intelligence, and, even more important, he has political power. Fowles's antipathy to Ayscough is evident in the narrator's criticisms of his bullying tactics and reactionary nature (227-28), but the author will not usurp the barrister's dominant position in the text. The bulk of it is structured in the question-and-answer format which he controls. The narrator speaks only in those briefer sections composed in the manner of a conventional novel, and even there his is just one of several limited perspectives. Fowles does not grant his narrator psychological and spatial omniscience. For example, the narrator is as much in the dark as the reader concerning the enigmatic motives and character of Bartholomew, and, as I have already said, the narrator is also ignorant of the crucially important happenings in the cave.

Novels such as *The Passion* and *A Maggot* self-consciously demonstrate that if the representation of history is not a purely disinterested or neutral activity, then genre plays a crucial role in determining its ideological shape (Lee 74). The eight novels examined here manifest traits associated with several genres and sub-genres, including the detective novel, the campus novel, the *Bildungsroman*, the romance, the gothic tale, and science fiction. All of these novels convey an awareness that genres are alterable cultural forms, not natural phenomena existing apart from human purposes. The treatment of genre in all, to one degree or another, is parodic in the sense defined by Hutcheon: in involving "repetition with critical distance that allows ironic signalling of difference at the very heart of similarity" (*Poetics* 26). In other words, the authors find ways to upset expectations about the requirements of works within a particular genre, and in the process to register a degree of scepticism about the capacity of the genre to represent experience adequately. Lee provides a good example in describing how *Star Turn* undermines the assumptions about the stability and continuity of individual identity upon which the *Bildungsroman* is based (60-62). As Lee shows, in his treatment of his central characters, Amos and Zak, Williams debunks rather than endorses the notion that the self is underpinned by an essential identity that evolves and grows over the course of life in a purposeful fashion. This is a topic upon which I shall expand in my fourth chapter, "History and Identity."

As I have already noted in discussing the textual heterogeneity which characterizes most of the eight novels, some of these works blend features of several genres in unstable or ambiguous combinations. These books bear out the contention of Vincent Leitch that "there is always genre but more than one, which is a methodological permutation of the claim that language is characterized by intertextuality and heteroglossia" (62-63). *The Passion*, for example, combines features of the realistic novel with those of the romance. Winterson assimilates a certain amount factual historical information about the Napoleonic wars into a narrative which often lacks plausibility on a realistic plane. But her method is somewhat paradoxical. She does not deploy the historical material and the conventions of realism in order to mask or minimize the implausible elements. Rather, like other novelists who work in the magic realist mode, Winterson employs the techniques of formal realism to give prominence to the marvellous features of the book. Individualizing touches and particularizing details make the fantastic seem concrete and real, but this is not the same as making it seem historically credible. What the reader of a conventional historical novel expects to see brought mimetically to life are "real" events and individuals, drawn from the documentary record, or at least ones that seem minimally compatible with known history, not episodes which seem more properly to belong to myths or folk tales.

An example of the way in which Winterson deploys magic realism is her treatment of the effect on Villanelle of her love affair with a married woman: so intense is Villanelle's passion that the woman is said to have stolen her heart, not just figuratively but literally. Henri is astounded to feel no heartbeat when Villanelle, who seems in excellent health, places his hand on her chest. Henri's quest to retrieve the stolen heart from the woman's house is described in considerable detail, right down to the stoppered, indigo jar wrapped in a silk shift in which the woman has hidden it (120). Henri describes the process by which Villanelle replaces her missing heart in concrete terms, as though it had what it patently could not have, a real physiological basis:

> I heard her uncork the jar and a sound like gas escaping. Then she began to make terrible swallowing and choking noises and only my fear kept me sitting at the other end of the boat, perhaps hearing her die.
>
> There was quiet. She touched my back and when I turned round took my hand again and placed it on her breast.
>
> Her heart was beating. (120-21)

The Passion's magic realism (like that of Angela Carter's *Nights at the Circus*) is designed to advance its feminist politics. Most of the fantastic elements are associated with Venice, a city which, in Winterson's hands, serves the cause of female liberation. Of course, the place is not without its misogynistic side, inasmuch as Villanelle's sex prevents her from following her heart's desire and becoming a boatman. As well, in this location she becomes the wife of a brutal man (significantly, though, a Frenchman, not a Venetian), who treats her as his chattel. Nevertheless, as an enchanted city, a "city of disguises" (56), Venice offers her the means to resist and escape oppression. Despite being a woman, she has been born with the webbed feet of Venetian boatmen, the magical feet which enable her to walk on water and so to pull the gondola carrying Henri to safety after they have lost their oars in their bloody fight with her vengeful husband (129). The amorphousness, mutability, and darkness of the place (its residents are said to have the night vision of cats [57]) provide her nooks in which to hide from her husband. "I lost myself in the dark that has always been a friend" (98), she says. This "invented city" (109), this "city of disguises" (56), enables her to attain a measure of freedom by embracing artifice and dressing as a man. Venice is also called one of the "cities of the interior [which] do not lie on any map" (114), an attribution which hints at why as a woman Villanelle feels perfectly home in it. The city is an objective correlative for what Winterson appears to see as a distinctively female psyche or "interior," one that disrupts the imperious rationality of patriarchy. Whether Winterson conceives of this feminine identity as culturally constructed or biologically based is unclear.

A Maggot is also generically complex in a way that produces tension and contradiction. Fowles's readers cannot activate one consistent set of codes with which to interpret the novel because it is by turns a detective story, a court-room drama, a historical study of numerous facets of eighteenth-century life, a lurid gothic tale, and a science-fiction adventure involving extra-terrestrials and a space ship. Such mixing of genres is a way of signalling the incomplete and unauthoritative nature of any one kind of narrative report.

Perhaps the most unsettling aspect of *A Maggot*'s proliferation of genres is the way in which the convention of realism applicable to historical fiction entailing a pose of documentary accuracy and fidelity to fact is confounded by the blatantly fantastic elements associated with gothic and science-fiction. Although elsewhere he has championed realism as a literary mode (Fowles and Halpern 36), the particular manner in which it is subverted in *A Maggot* suggests that Fowles might want to demonstrate what has become a commonplace charge in the wake of French structuralism: that belief in the transparency of language, and in the positivist assumptions bound up with it, masks a destructive ideology. At least one could infer that he intends this pejorative association from his treatment of the hateful Henry Ayscough, whose relentless application of the scientific method in his investigation into the mysterious disappearance of the young aristocrat Bartholomew is expressly used as an instrument of an oppressive social order. His conduct in eliciting testimony from various witnesses leaves no doubt that he believes that language, when used honestly, corresponds simply and directly to a reality which is nothing more than the conservative world view of the ruling class of his time. Since the investigative methods by which he would solve the mystery are highly redolent of those employed in detective novels, *A Maggot* corroborates Lee's claim that this sort of fiction "is an innately conservative genre" and that the detective is "a guardian of ideology" (67).

I am not saying that Fowles, or indeed any of the other seven novelists, would crudely equate all literary realism with bourgeois political bad faith. It is true that all of the novelists included in my study expose the limits of realism and deflate the most grandiose claims which have been made for it, but this does not mean that they dismiss it entirely or assume that it will always constitute, in the words of Roland Barthes, "a totalitarian ideology of the referent" ("To Write" 138). As Andrzej Gąsiorek argues, "realisms" are multiple, not single, and they "can no more be equated with a particular political stance than with a given set of narrative strategies" (4-5). That none of the eight novelists totally repudiates the realist tradition is shown in the fact that all of them strive for realistic effects of one kind or another in excess of what would be needed merely to create a simulacrum of "reality" that could subsequently be undermined. The essential point here is that attempts to achieve verisimilitude do not necessarily serve a belief that there is consensus about the nature of reality or that language is unproblematically capable of mirroring it. As Waugh accurately points out, "most realist novels involve modes of irony and linguistic playfulness which are ignored in many of the theoretical formulations of Realism" (*Practising Postmodernism* 58). In this context, too, it is worth repeating what Malcolm Bradbury wrote several years ago: "realism . . . is not necessarily an antithesis to experiment, nor a self-evidently unspeculative mode" (174).

CHAPTER THREE

Attitudes to the Past

This third chapter analyzes the assumptions about the nature of history which emerge from the events narrated in the novels and the responses of the characters to them. Broadly speaking, there are two contradictory attitudes, based on whether the processes of historical change are experienced as damaging or nourishing. The first is a broadly tragic view which is expressed succinctly in Jameson's well known aphorism that "[h]istory is what hurts." He adds that "it is what refuses desire and sets inexorable limits to individual as well as collective praxis, which its 'ruses' turn into grisly and ironic reversals of their overt intention" (*Political Unconscious* 102). This is history as the modernists experienced it: as Joyce's nightmare or Eliot's "immense panorama of futility and anarchy" (177). It is loss of community, predatory capitalist social relations, and the shattering of beliefs, whether in God, rationality, or the unitary self. But preeminently, it is history as anarchic violence and war. The traumatic effect of the Great War on *Star Turn*'s narrator, Amos Barking, for example, is merely a ghastly prelude to the horrific impact on him of later events with which he has first-hand experience, such as the rise of fascism in Britain and the fire-bombing of Dresden. Williams's treatment of the First World War in relation to subsequent events of the first half of the twentieth century squares in every detail with Perkins's observation that the war's significance beyond its immediately destructive effects was to disclose "the modal facts that reveal the essence of the human condition; extreme physical horror; violence; omnipresent death; the meaninglessness and futility of individual effort; the feeling that man is subject to an invisible, apparently insane bureaucracy; the blind turmoil of history shattering private life" (*History of Modern Poetry* 1:268).

Most of the novels reflect in one way or another this familiarly apocalyptic picture of modern history. *Moon Tiger*'s Claudia, for instance, calls ours the "century of war. All history, of course, is the history of wars, but this hundred years has excelled itself. How many million shot, maimed, burned, frozen, starved, drowned?" (66). As Claudia says, it is not merely the recent past which has been blighted by war. Winterson's grim depiction of the Napoleonic wars seems paradigmatic in much the same way that Williams's evocation of the two twentieth-century world wars does. However differently wars were fought in past eras, however much they were imbued with religious or chivalric or nationalistic ideals, their results were the same: carnage, devastation, and suffering. Violence is an enduring fact of life, as is mortality. And because mortality is a universal condition, history can seem apocalyptic to people of any epoch (Kermode 95). *A History of the World in 10 1/2 Chapters* features the recurrent metaphor of human history, from its very beginnings to the present, as a desperate voyage by a boat or ship on which people are seeking deliverance from various kinds of catastrophes. These vessels range from the aforementioned biblical Ark and nineteenth-century frigate *Medusa* to twentieth-century ocean liners such as the *Titanic* and the *St. Louis*, which in 1939 carried a cargo of Jewish refugees from Nazi Germany to ports in many countries which refused to admit them.

Some of the novels, though, at least consider a degenerative model in which history, rather than being uniformly blighted over its entire course, has declined in some respects from earlier periods in which the possibilities for various kinds of fulfillment were greater. Both *Chatterton* and *A Maggot* explore the eighteenth-century origins of Romantic sensibility, and both communicate longing for the imaginative scope of their eighteenth-century protagonists. This longing accounts for Wychwood's obsession with Chatterton and with the novel's presentation of his forgeries as works of great invention. "Thus do we see in every line an Echoe," writes Ackroyd's Chatterton, "for the truest Plagiarism is the truest Poetry" (87). In the case of *A Maggot*, Rebecca Lee's imaginative acuity makes her a story-telling surrogate for Fowles himself, as is made clear by his comments on the Shakers, the religious movement which he imagines to have been founded upon her visionary experience: "Something in Shaker thought and theology . . . has always seemed to me to adumbrate the relation of fiction to reality. We novelists also demand a far-fetched faith, quite often seemingly absurd in relation to normal reality; we too need a bewildering degree of metaphorical understanding from our readers before the truths behind our tropes can be conveyed" (450-51).

As did Fowles's earlier work *The French Lieutenant's Woman*, *Possession* and *Ever After* both exploit the nostalgia pervasive in British high brow culture for the Victorian past, with its unambiguous social hierarchy, its reassuringly solid and densely cluttered interiors, its seeming confidence, stability, and unclouded sense of purpose. The twentieth-century characters in the novels by Byatt and Swift look to the nineteenth-century figures in whom they are interested to supply qualities lacking in their own lives and societies. I have already intimated that Swift's Bill Unwin, in his despair, turns for solace to his ancestor Matthew and his seemingly more secure Victorian world. Byatt's unfulfilled modern academics envy the Victorian poets whom they are studying for the intensity and vitality of their inner lives. The intimacy of mind and feeling that develops between Ash and LaMotte as they correspond contrasts with the furtiveness and dishonesty that characterize Roland's relationship with Val and with the sexual and intellectual predacity that damaged Maud's relationship with Fergus Wolff. Separated from the Victorians by the chasm dug by Freud, Roland and Maud long nostalgically for the great age of humanism before the splintering of the unitary self. "They valued themselves," says Maud of the Victorians. "Once, they knew God valued them. Then they began to think there was no God, only blind forces. So they valued themselves, they loved themselves and attended to their natures—" (254).

This harkening back to a better time as an anodyne for the pains inflicted by history may ultimately be a search for origins, for God, for some fundamental principle or pattern which has been abandoned or lost. Certainly, Byatt's Ash and LaMotte seem to Roland and Maud to be closer to some basic truth about life's meaning. For the Victorian pair, imaginative empathy and romantic love—which their modern counterparts have learned to mistrust as "a suspect ideological construct" (267) —are a means of getting in touch with this archetypal reality. Here, for example, are Randolph's thoughts and feelings as he meditates on the significance of Christabel's waist:

> He thought of her momentarily as an hour-glass containing time. . . . She held his time, she contained his past and his future, both now cramped together, with such ferocity and such gentleness, into this small circumference. He remembered an odd linguistic fact—the word for waist in Italian is *vita*, is life. . . . This is my centre, he thought, here, at this place, at this time, in her, in that narrow place, where my desire has its end.   (287)

The need to tap the primordial origins of existence is what motivates Randolph's interest in biology and paleontology. It accounts as well for his and Christabel's fascination with the mythological stories, folk tales, and fairy tales that permeate the novel. Though living in an age of science, the two poets effortlessly imbue their relationship with an aura of the fabulous derived from an earlier, more "primitive" age. For example, Ash perceives LaMotte, living in seclusion, as the Lady of Shalott or as the fairy Melusina, hedged about with prohibition, and he sees himself riding in the park toward her cottage as a knight undertaking a timeless journey:

I had the sensation . . . that I was moving out of time, . . . and that I was who I had been and what I would become—all at once, all wound in one. . . . Now to me such moments are poetry. Do not misunderstand me—I do not mean missishly "poetical"— but the source of the driving force of the lines—And when I write lines I mean the lines of verse indeed, but also some lines of life which run indifferently through us—from Origin to Finish. (182)

For characters in two of Barnes's fictions, this search for a better past takes the form of a physical trek to the fabled resting place of Noah's Ark, Turkey's Mount Ararat, undertaken in the hope of receiving a divine revelation with which to counter the threat to religion posed by science. These characters find in Noah's story the origins of a renewing, providential design, which his forbears have foolishly lost sight of in an era of secularism and materialism. The Ark, of course, signifies deliverance. But the nineteenth-century Amanda Ferguson of "The Mountain," whose religious dogmatism masks an insecurity bred by debates with her late father, only ostensibly ascends the mountain to petition God to forgive him for his atheism. In reality, she hungers for a sign that God will ignore His covenant with humankind and destroy all those who fail to meet the standards of her severe faith. In "Project Ararat," the twentieth-century astronaut Spike Tiggler, heeding the instruction of a disembodied voice which he heard on the moon, sets out more than a century after Amanda's pilgrimage to find the remains of Noah's Ark. Like Amanda, Spike is "looking for where we came from" (262). Both are ultimately searching for incontestable evidence of God's reality as our source.

Of course, the authors whose works I am studying are too sophisticated and sceptical to subscribe wholeheartedly to a "golden age" myth. Spike fervently believes that he discovers Noah's skeleton on Ararat, but, when carbon dating proves that the bones are those of a woman who died only a century or so before, readers know that what Spike has unearthed is the corpse of Amanda from "The Mountain." In that earlier story, after injuring herself (seemingly deliberately), she remains alone in a cave on Ararat in the sure belief that this suicidal decision is the will of a God who is poised to save her. We do not doubt the reality of her belief that she is acquiescing in God's original purpose (in contrast, her father, with his Victorian faith in progress, set his sights on "the way forward" [145], not the way back), but Barnes puts the reader at an ironic remove from her and her modern counterpart, Spike. What

Barnes does implicitly affirm is not the existence of God or some providential design but rather the importance of religious beliefs in the movement of history. The comments of *Moon Tiger*'s Claudia about the place of God in history provide a useful gloss: "God shall have a starring role in my history of the world. How could it be otherwise? If He exists, then He is responsible for the whole marvellous appalling narrative. If He does not, then the very proposition that He might has killed more people and exercised more minds than anything else. He dominates the stage" (56). The documentary record leaves no doubt that religious beliefs dictate events, but, Barnes's stories suggest, it cannot validate the truth of those beliefs by verifying the reality of God as the force behind history.

The novels by Fowles, Ackroyd, Swift, and Byatt also subvert the notion that the past really was superior to the present. Fowles and Ackroyd may, as I have said, admire the incipient Romanticism of their protagonists, Rebecca Lee and Thomas Chatterton respectively, but they also undermine its credibility by enveloping them both in ambiguity. Yes, both characters are visionaries with prodigious imaginations, but their veracity is questionable. Chatterton perpetrates fraud and Lee tells stories which might not be true. Byatt and Swift show that upon close scrutiny our envied Victorian forbears can be seen to have suffered from the same epistemological and existential difficulties which afflict us. *Possession*'s Ash, for instance, does not often feel in touch with an original reality. Most of the time, just like the novel's modern scholars, he believes himself to be problematically removed from such a source:

> The truth is — my dear Miss Lamotte — that we live in an old world — a world that has gone on piling up speculation and observations until truths that might have been graspable in the bright Dayspring of human morning — by the young Plotinus or the ecstatic John of Patmos — are now obscured by palimpsest on palimpsest, by thick horny growths over that clear vision. (164)

Despite the failure of the glorified past to stand up to rigorous investigation, the novels suggest that this kind of idealization is a powerful, recurrent urge. Although Ash's Victorian age is glorified by some of the modern characters, as the passage quoted above shows, he himself, ironically, indulges in the same elevation of an even more distant past. The same tendency is displayed by Fowles's Bartholomew, a magus-like figure whose era is held up by Fowles to be less fettered than our own in some respects. Nevertheless, Bartholomew lionizes the freedom, innocence and wisdom of the prehistoric builders of Stonehenge (an important setting in *A Maggot*). "Then he gestured about us, at the stones," testifies one of Bartholomew's minions about the young aristocrat, "and said, Do you not admire that, perhaps before Rome, before Christ Himself, these savages who set these stones knew something even our Newtons and Leibnitzes cannot reach?" (143).

The sense that historical continuity with a desired past has been severed is a familiar refrain in the literature of our century, particularly in the works of modernist writers. Think, for example, of Virginia Woolf's famous contrast between her fragmented society, which had condemned the writer to "the cramp and confinement of personality," and Jane Austen's England, with its reassuring social consensus about values (302). Or think of Eliot's theory concerning the impoverishing "dissociation of sensibility" which, he believed, occurred during the seventeenth century and continued to affect authors right up to his own day (64). The need to posit a schismatic fall into modernity has seemingly not been weakened by the failure of writers to agree on its exact character or on the precise historical point at which the event took place.

The desire to overcome the abyss and achieve continuity with vanished traditions and patterns of thought and feeling accounts for the way in which historical activity is treated in some of the novels which I have singled out. That is, the processes of historical reconstruction themselves become attempts to bridge the gap and reconstitute the lost past. Representation thus becomes a substitute for a living connection to what is prized in bygone eras. All of the novels signal this intent quite self-consciously in that their protagonists draw attention to it by becoming their authors' surrogates in the quest to inscribe the reality of the past. What I said in Chapter One about *A Maggot* is equally true of the other works: they focus attention on history not only by containing episodes set in the historical past but also by featuring characters' attempts to reconstruct the past. Many of the characters themselves, then, act as historians of a kind, even though Lively's Claudia and Barnes's Franklin Hughes (of "The Visitors") are the only professional historians of the group. Ackroyd's Charles Wychwood, Byatt's modern academics, and Swift's Bill Unwin try to discover in the lives of long-dead individuals patterns of narrative coherence and unity which can attach to and give meaning to their own troubled situations.

However, the novels frustrate their efforts by bringing to the fore the problematics of representation, by showing that their endeavours say as much as or more about their own contemporary circumstances than they do about the real nature of the past, which cannot be recuperated. For example, in trying to understand the seventeenth-century Puritans who sailed to North America on the *Mayflower*, Lively's Claudia conducts a mental dialogue with them and in the process comments succinctly on the insuperable difficulty of historicism: "And I know, also, nothing. Because I cannot shed my skin and put on yours, cannot strip my mind of its knowledge and its prejudices, cannot look cleanly at the world with the eyes of a child, am as imprisoned by my time as you were by yours" (31). In this regard, one could also instantiate Bill Unwin's revelation in *Ever After* that design is something projected onto the past rather than discovered in it. He becomes aware that the tradition of seeing in history a purposeful shape formed by the activities of "Great Men" such as Charles Darwin is blind to the contingencies behind events, even those which led to Darwin's momentous discoveries. Ironically, Unwin sees the randomness which plays so central a role in Darwin's theory of natural selection as the decisive element in the Victorian biologist's own career and, by implication, in the movement of history itself (237-39).

The revelation that historical representations are necessarily distortions of a past whose real character can never be objectively transmitted is obviously unsettling in the context of the pursuit of continuity. But it has a paradoxically beneficial use which some of the novels explore. If the antiquarian aim to reconstruct past ages in all of their plenitude is quixotic, then perhaps "presentism" will serve equally well. If our recorded images of the past are all so partial and coloured by our limited perspectives as to be, in effect, fictive, then perhaps we can shape them to serve current ends without worrying that we are dishonestly misrepresenting the objective reality of the past, which in any event we have no access to. If, as Ackroyd's eccentric novelist Harriet Slope contends, history is "the one thing we have to make up for ourselves" (226), then it doesn't matter that the documents on which Charles Wychwood based his theory about Chatterton were forged, since all of the documents in the intertextual web which comprise the historical archive are unreliable in any event. What matters, according to Philip Slack, in conversation with Charles's widow, Vivien, is the power of the fiction to inspire belief: "We can keep the belief alive. . . . The important thing is what Charles imagined, and we can keep hold of that. That isn't an illusion. The imagination never dies" (232). Readers might be tempted to ask how a belief can be kept alive once it has been exposed as baseless, but the novel does seem to corroborate Slack's position on the power of the imagination. Chatterton mysteriously appears in the present on two occasions, apparently in response to Charles's intense imaginative empathy with him.

This same historiographical tactic—adapting our images of the past to our needs in the present—can be applied to aspects of the past which are frightening as well as to those which are comforting or attractive in some way. It might seem paradoxical to want to represent and in the process experience (or re-experience, in the case of very recent history) events which are disturbing, but such activity can be a way of imposing order upon and making more manageable processes which are chaotic and threatening. In such cases, it is history as lived experience which "hurts" (in Jameson's formulation), and historical representation is motivated by the need to distance the past, not to make it live again in all of its vividness. This is unmistakably the motive of *Star Turn*'s Amos Barking, whose employment as a propagandist during the Second World War is entirely compatible with his belief that it is impossible to record history with objective accuracy. That his farcical evocations of minatory historical figures such as Douglas Haig and Joseph Goebbels lack verisimilitude is beside the point; what is important is that the caricatures defuse the menace of these individuals. Believing as he does that the writing of history is a kind of fictionalizing (250), Barking tries to use the fictions to defend his psyche from the buffets of the historical events which engulf him and ultimately destroy his friend Isaac Rabinowitz. "I am determined to enjoy the illusion of control," he thinks. "There are things out there that are determined to control *me*" (197).

In considering the status of imagination in relation to the treatment of historiography in *Chatterton* and *Star Turn*, I have begun to encroach somewhat on a topic that I shall examine in more detail in the last chapter of this book. It suffices here to say that, for Williams and the other novelists in question, "presentism" ultimately proves as deficient as antiquarianism in the representation of history. What Hutcheon claims generally about postmodernism is true of these particular novels: "For the most part historiographic metafiction, like much contemporary theory of history, does not fall into either 'presentism' or nostalgia in its relation to the past it represents. . . . In both historiographical and literary postmodern representation, the doubleness remains; there is no sense of either historian or novelist reducing the strange past to verisimilar present" (*Politics* 71).

All of the novels insist on the importance of the epistemological barrier which separates the present from the past, but both antiquarian nostalgia and "presentism" ignore or eradicate that barrier. Antiquarian nostalgia entails the belief that we can leave the present to inhabit the full reality of the past. Such an aim leads to what LaCapra calls "over-contextualization," which "occurs when one so immerses a text in the particularities of its own time and place that one impedes responsive understanding and excessively restricts the interaction between past and present" (132). The opposite danger, "presentism," assumes that present interpretations or uses of whatever remains of the past are all that matter. Antiquarianism is too naive to be tenable, and "presentism," as Bennett says, renders the notion of history meaningless: "[Historical] debates require, as a condition of their intelligibility, the sense of a distinction between past and present and an orientation to historical records *as if* they comprised a referent. That this referent proves to be intra-discursive and so mutable does not disable the historical enterprise" (50-51).

Despite Bennett's subsequent claim that "the cogency and productivity of historical inquiry may be admitted without the question of its relations to 'the real past' ever arising" (51), to be meaningful historical debates also require the presupposition that the occurrences of the past had an independent reality to which the documents in the archive bear some relation. Hutcheon's distinction between "the brute *events* of the past and the historical *facts* that we construct out of them" is germane here. "Facts are events to which we have given meaning" (*Politics* 57). As Mink says in the passage which I quoted in Chapter One, we can never have unmediated access to those events, as though they constituted "the untold story to which narrative histories approximate" (202). Our historical facts, accordingly, will lack a hard foundation, but that does not mean that we are free to construct them in any way that we like. That our facts are our own inventions does not logically imply that they do not also refer to states of affairs separate from our mental processes.

It might be consoling in some situations to pretend that we can fabricate the past in any way that we like, but abandoning the quest for historical truths—however multiple and provisional—can have implications that are morally disturbing. One thinks of Lenny in Pinter's *The Homecoming*, who, after alleging that he has beaten and contemplated killing a prostitute for offering him sex, justifies his action by saying that she had venereal disease. His response to Ruth's question concerning how he knew the woman was diseased is chilling in a way that is obviously pertinent to the issue at hand: "I decided she was" (31). The narrator of Barnes's "Parenthesis" provides what could serve as a criticism of this attempt to pass off might for right:

> We all know that objective truth is not attainable, that when some event occurs we shall have a multiplicity of subjective truths which we assess and then fabulate into history, into some God-eyed version of what "really"

happened. This God-eyed version is a fake—a charming, impossible fake. . . . But while we know this, we must still believe that objective truth is obtainable; or we must believe that it is 99 per cent obtainable; or if we can't believe this we must believe that 43 per cent objective truth is better than 41 per cent. We must do so, because if we don't we're lost, we fall into beguiling relativity, we value one liar's version as much as another liar's, we throw up our hands at the puzzle of it all, we admit that the victor has the right not just to the spoils but also to the truth.   (243-44)

Williams's Barking comments in a similar vein when he repudiates his own practice of ignoring or distorting evidence while fabricating his narratives: "Things happen. Whether they happened or not can be tested and discovered. To abandon that hope is to abandon hope in any kind of justice or decency. What happened last night happened" (307). The last sentence refers to the bombing of Dresden, the horror of which constrains the range of interpretations that he can derive from it. He is unable to turn that horror into nationalistic propaganda in support of Britain's war effort. His last words in the novel, a cry of anguish, confess his failure as a writer to make modern history fit the contour of his own desires: "Make it all go away, somebody, can't you?" (314).

Although we lack consensus about its objective meanings, history is a force which, in the eight novels studied here, will not be made to go away; it cannot, in the final analysis, be wholly banished, neutralized or transcended. But it is going too far to say of these works, as Hutcheon does of postmodernism generally, that they do not allow us "to stand outside history, or even to wish to do so" (*Poetics* 88). Amos Barking would clearly like to do so, and presumably Nigel Williams shares this wish, at least in certain moods. Moreover, as we saw in the previous chapter, some of the novels do suggest that, in certain senses, we sometimes "stand outside history," or at least that it is less rigid and constricting than it is often taken to be. As Hutcheon herself allows (88), the distinction between the modernist desire to evade history and the postmodernist one to engage with it is not absolute by any means. If modernist writers turned for protection to the aesthetic realm and attempted to treat art as a self-contained timeless space, they sometimes acknowledged that the processes of historical change had invaded the sanctuary. Does not, for example, the prominent role of contingency in *Ulysses* amount to such an acknowledgment? And might not Woolf's *Orlando*, to take a second example, be seen not as a triumph of poetic form which denies the reality of English history but, in the novel's playful, parodic treatment of periodization, as a postmodernist recognition that our historical narratives and the concepts with which we make

57

sense of the past are human constructions which sometimes serve broadly political goals? And if postmodernist writers tend to be, in their ironic treatment of the aesthetic resources at their disposal, less than reverent believers in the religion of art, they sometimes express a longing for the consolations which have been denied them.

The narrator of Part II of Barnes's "Shipwreck," for instance, lauds the process by which Theodore Géricault in painting *The Raft of the Medusa* "turn[ed] catastrophe into art" (125) by eliminating the political considerations involved in the shipwreck and allowing "questions of form [to] predominate" in his representation (135): "Catastrophe has become art; but this is no reducing process. It is freeing, enlarging, explaining. Catastrophe has become art: that is, after all, what it is for" (137). But though he admires the victory, Barnes feels obliged to reverse or at least subvert it by situating the painting historically. He provides a précis of the excluded political struggle between Bonapartists and monarchists, thereby reminding us of the specific social context in which the painting was originally conceived, executed, and received by the viewing public, and he also describes the messiness and contingencies of the artistic process which Géricault followed in the sketches which preceded the painting. Barnes concludes the short fiction by deflating the traditional ideal of art's immortality, however much he might like to subscribe to it himself:

> And there we have it—the moment of supreme agony on the raft, taken up, transformed, justified by art, turned into a sprung and weighted image, then varnished, framed, glazed, hung in a famous gallery to illuminate our human condition, fixed, final, always there. Is that what we have? Well, no. People die; rafts rot; and works of art are not exempt. . . . Our leading expert on Géricault confirms that the painting is "now in part a ruin." (130)

CHAPTER FOUR

History and Identity

All of the novels examined here reflect, in one way or another, the widely discussed crisis of subjectivity in contemporary culture. Particularly relevant in this regard are the attacks on traditional liberal humanist notions of selfhood, launched by figures such as Barthes, Derrida, Lacan, Kristeva, Althusser, and Foucault. In some intellectual circles it goes almost without saying that the unified, integral self who is capable of moral choices and purposive historical action is a mirage fabricated by totalizing discourses, such as those of the traditional novel or history. This identity is held to be the product of the same ideology (capitalist and patriarchal) which it is designed to mask. According to Anthony Easthope, this conception of selfhood involves a Cartesian separation of subject and object which leads to a wholly destructive use of intellect: "the emergence and persistence of the classical subject has come to be understood as in every respect aggressive and exploitive: assuming itself to be as self-originating as God, it is constituted in the need to appropriate everything other than itself to its own avowed self-sufficiency as origin of power and knowledge" (63). Waugh elaborates: "Reason, even in its Enlightenment mode, is . . . seen as part of the impulse to control and subjugate which is the logic of capitalism and which has led to the violent forms of oppression in the modern world: imperialism, colonialism, racism, sexism, destruction of the environment, automatization of human beings for the purposes of efficiency" (*Practising Postmodernism* 74).

The rational subject of liberal humanism, straw man that he has become, clearly has a lot to answer for. Without denying the reality of either the evils mentioned above or the exclusions, inadequacies, and contradictions in the humanist image of humanity, I would want to add that Western Man has no monopoly on "violent forms of oppression"; that instrumental reason and its technologies have been and are being used all over the world to benefit people as well as to exploit them; that arguments about the role of ideologies in the formation of identity which dismiss opposed views in advance as the products of those same ideologies appear suspiciously tautological and self-serving; and that it is entirely possible to resist rather than to promote the "automatization of human beings for the purposes of efficiency" on the basis of a humanist belief in the innate dignity of our species. Laurence Lerner is worth attending to when he says that the "picture of a black slave with the subscription 'Am I not also a man and a brother?' is a reminder that radicalism often appeals to an ideal of humanity that, instead of articulating existing power relations, deliberately offers itself in contrast to them" (275). The current privileging in much theoretical writing of what is concrete, situated, particular and local (Liu 77) has blinded us to the fact that, without broad political or ethical ideals that cut across the lines of gender or race or nationality which divide particular groups of people from each other, the claim that some groups have been exploited or marginalized is meaningless. In the absence of such values, appeals to justice are beside the point; the only meaningful consideration is whether any given group has the power to exert its political will over other groups.

The problem, however, is the absence of a firm authority for any set of values or norms which could underwrite a universally accepted model of human identity. The eight novels on which I am concentrating all exhibit a tension between an urge to uncover some essential or enduring truth about existence and an awareness that such a goal is belied by the relative, contingent nature of experience. All the books reveal a conflict between a desire to see the self as integrated (or at least as capable of being so) and a postmodernist tendency to see it as decentered and fragmented. In themselves, the methods of characterization in the majority of these works are not so radical (after the fashion, say, of some of Donald Barthelme's) as to prevent us from conceiving of the protagonists as representations of people possessing underlying, if elusive, individual identities, but they undergo experiences which subvert our ability to see them in this way.

Major characters in most of these books suffer crises of identity, brought on, in nearly every case, by destructive historical forces. Winterson's Henri, for example, loses his equilibrium and is ultimately driven into madness following the defeat of the political ideal embodied in Napoleon, with whom he had identified totally. He subsequently turns for support to Villanelle, who is unable to reciprocate his passion and so sustain his fragile sense of self. "Wordlessly, she explains me to myself" (122), he tells us hopefully, but Villanelle rejects as incompatible with her own highly fluid, multiple identities the kind of exclusive, heterosexual relationship upon which Henri's self image seems to depend. Swift's Bill Unwin, too, who is recovering from an attempted suicide, is shattered by the failure of love to supply an enduring definition of self. The deaths, first of his father and then of his wife, Ruth, who "held things together for [him], who held [his] world together" (125), make him morbidly sensitive to the transitoriness of individual identity in the face of mortality. Another character who breaks down psychologically is the desperate narrator of Barnes's "The Survivor," a woman so overwhelmed emotionally by the threat of nuclear disaster and the degradation of the natural environment that she flees civilization in a small boat. Finally, the emotionally incapacitated Zak Rabinovitch of *Star Turn* is treated by "Sigmund Freud" after political events cause him to lose faith in the Marxist values which have animated him.

The vulnerability of the self to disintegration is hardly the discovery of postmodernism. In fact, Jameson claims that it is more characteristically the concern of modernist authors, who frequently express anxiety over the readiness of individual identity to break down in "Van Gogh-type madness." For Jameson, this psychic fragility is allied with modernist alienation, not postmodernist fragmentation (*Postmodernism* 14). Nevertheless, psychological breakdowns of the sort discussed above could be viewed as consonant with the emphasis in postmodernism on identity as an artificial construct rather than as something elemental and secure which precedes the individual's social interactions. Most of the novels do, as it happens, contain overt commentary supporting the idea that personal identity is the mutable product of transitory historical phases, not an autonomous entity which transcends them.

Fowles's narrator in *A Maggot,* for example, states explicitly that modern ideas of subjectivity are a consequence of the historical forces which produced individualism; he says of one of his eighteenth-century characters, Rebecca Lee's husband, that "he still lacks what even the least intelligent human today, far stupider even than he, would recognize—an unmistakable sense of personal identity set in a world to some degree, however small, manipulable or controllable by that identity. John Lee would not have understood *Cogito, ergo sum*; and far less its even terser modern equivalent, I am" (385). The modern protagonists of *Possession* subscribe to the poststructuralist theory that the various roles that make up an individual's subjectivity are the products of language and other sign systems. Roland Michell, for instance, "had learned to see himself, theoretically, as a crossing place for a number of systems, all loosely connected. He had been trained to see his idea of his 'self' as an illusion, to be replaced by a discontinuous machinery and electrical message network of various desires, ideological beliefs and responses, language-forms and hormones and pheromones" (424). As I mentioned in the previous chapter, the romantic love which fails securely to underpin the identities of Winterson's Henri and Swift's Bill Unwin is for Roland and Maud one of those "suspect ideological construct[s]" (267). *Ever After*'s Bill Unwin, as well, recognizes that the love upon which his sense of self has been founded may actually be a transient product of history rather than a timeless bulwark against its ravages: "Romantic love. A made-up thing. A concoction of the poets" (121).

Bill illustrates a highly paradoxical response to the dilemma outlined above in that he turns to history to try to repair the damage of history. His psychological crisis, which seems to be exclusively personal, is actually directly attributable to the historical forces which have shaped the lives of his immediate family. The Second World War and its aftermath are critical in this regard, since the suicide of his father might have been caused by the man's guilt over the secret role which he played in the development of nuclear weapons (204-05). The traumatic effect on Bill of this suicide cannot be overemphasized: "I am my father's son," he tells us, ". . . by whose death my life has been so irreversibly moulded" (171-72). Rather than trying to cast off this sad legacy and invent himself afresh, Bill turns to an even more distant past to look for the seeds of a true identity. The notion that the paradigm of his authentic self can be found in the lives of his forbears is what fuels his interest in his family's history. Finally, it is to his great-great-grandfather, Matthew Pearce, that Bill turns in his quest for an alter ego, not to the man who raised him as his father nor to his biological father (Bill learns belatedly that his real father was not the decorated veteran who shot himself but a nameless engine driver, killed in the war, with whom his mother had an extra-marital affair): "I summon up Matthew, but I do not try to know my own father. . . . And why should I, when I never got to know the living, breathing man whom I took to be—?" (219).

It is highly ironic that Bill hopes to save himself by immersing himself in the documentary record of his ancestor's life, because Matthew, like Bill, suffered an existential crisis. The death of his son Felix, following hard upon the loss of his religious faith, struck at the heart of his own sense of self and eventually led to the breakup of his marriage. In answer to Elizabeth's entreaty to "call upon [his] better nature and 'be [himself] again,'" Matthew, in his journal, reports thinking the following: "'Better Nature'? What, in any of us is our 'better nature'? And what does it mean . . . to 'be oneself'?" (225). Although stability is the hallmark of Bill's initial presentation of Matthew and his Victorian world, Bill is always aware that its seemingly stable foundation will soon crumble. In fact, Matthew and his nineteenth-century milieu attract Bill precisely *because* he can see his own troubled situation in their mirror, but that very similarity militates against his being able to discover in the past the stability which he craves. The latter part of the nineteenth century, as Matthew's plight shows, was the very time when order and stability were being placed in jeopardy. Feeling a slave to destructive social forces that have warped his development, Bill turns for liberation, ironically, to a figure who was equally shaped, and marred, by history. For Matthew's crisis of faith was a typical, even a clichéd, experience for an educated Victorian, not one which set him apart as unique and self-directing. Through such pointedly ironic details, Swift invites us to view Bill's search for an original core of identity located in the past as quixotic.

If, as the examples of Bill and Matthew show, the self is a product of history as much as of biology, then it is not available as a refuge from history's depredations. Some of the novels under consideration here depict the failure of characters to withdraw into a private mental haven untouched by the forces moulding the larger, public world. The best example is *Star Turn*'s Amos Barking, whose spectatorial disengagement from and ironic perspective on historical events testify to his desire to separate his inner being from them. But the outer chaos keeps breaking through his psychic defenses; he admits this, echoing Joyce: "I don't understand my history or the history of my times. It is some kind of nightmare for me, from which I am unable to awake" (167).

His friend Zak, as the victim of anti-Semitism, also tries to preserve his ego from the ravages of his environment, but he does this not by attempting to retreat into some inviolable part of himself but by "us[ing] fantasy for tactical purposes" (38), by fashioning a succession of personae which he hopes are strong enough to confront and master the threat. Whereas Amos wants to keep history at arm's length by recording it, Zak wants to control it through direct action. "The boy wants to make history" (45), his father says. Zak continually fails, though, and over time he comes to see that his changing roles emanate, not from his private imagination, but from history itself: "'You must embrace the stupidity of the times,' said Isaac. 'When they are hysterical you must sob and laugh with them, when the time comes to be serious— put on your solemn face. Act it out. Act it out. This history of yours is nothing but a performance'" (248). It is a gruesome irony that he is beaten to death while impersonating a figure who embodies all that he has feared, the fascist Oswald Mosley. Far from making history, then, Zak is destroyed by it, having been "subjected to the manipulation of the social forces he trie[d] to master" (Lee 63). Lee is astute in noting that not only Zak but also *Star Turn*'s other characters "are subjected to the manifestations of history and politics rather than being in control of them" (66).

Just as Williams's characterization of Zak dissolves the boundary between the individual's private mental world and the public realm of impersonal historical events, so does Lively's depiction of Claudia Hampton. But *Moon Tiger* presents a far more optimistic interpretation of the relationship between history and individual identity than does *Star Turn*. Zak is a mere puppet, a fragmented, fully postmodern subject who is constrained to enact an incoherent succession of roles dictated by transient political and cultural phenomena. Claudia, however, feels that she is made complete by the public, historical dimension of her being, which is what connects her to the universe at large. "[U]nless I am part of everything I am nothing," she says (207). Zak is diminished, even extinguished, by history, whereas Claudia is made greater by it. "Like everything else," she says of one of the historical periods about which she has written, "it enlarges me, it frees me from the prison of my experience; it also resounds within that experience" (159). Claudia thus conceives of her own subjectivity as a blend in which private and public aspects inform and complete one another. She has, in a broad sense, been formed by history, but her identity, once shaped, nevertheless has a private aspect. In other words, this private dimension is created by historical forces, not obliterated by them. In turn, this self turns purposely and actively back to history (both lived and recorded) in quest of growth and fulfillment. Rather than being absorbed by history, then, she absorbs it within her private being: "You are public property—the received past. But you are also private; my view of you is my own, your relevance to me is personal" (29).

Mary Moran comes close to expressing Lively's point of view here in noting that "Claudia believes that an individual life embodies world history both in the sense that one is who one is because of all that happened before and in the sense that history does not exist apart from the individual contemplating it" (91). The one qualification I would make here is the obvious point that, in affirming that the historical past is "public property," Lively is not saying that history is entirely the subjective creation of the individual. It would be more accurate to say that she implies that any individual's awareness of the historical past will inevitably have a selective, highly subjective aspect. Germane in this regard is Claudia's reference to "the confection of fact and fantasy that is how we know the world" (62).

The difference between *Moon Tiger*'s Claudia and *Star Turn*'s Zak is that Claudia believes that at the deepest level she possesses something very like an essential self, whereas Zak's multiple personae are all externally derived and unessential. Moran (92) notes that Claudia uses geological metaphors to describe her "core" or "vital centre," which contrasts with her more peripheral "strata" (12). This core, like the strata, is acquired during the course of life rather than being inborn, like a soul in the Judeo-Christian tradition. This is evident in the fact that Claudia conceives of her dead lover Tom Southern, whom she did not meet until she was fully grown, as her core. Other, less significant individuals in her life, such as her husband Jasper and her daughter Lisa, comprise the strata.

This sense of a core identity serves Claudia as a source stability and fulfillment which is conspicuously absent in Zak's life. Zak's fate gives the lie to some of the positive claims that have been made for the fluid, indeterminate, free-floating postmodernist self. Richard Poirier lauds the "performing self" as a liberation from the constraining values of liberal humanism and more generally from all pre-existing structures (xv), but Zak's performances lack the creative energy Poirier speaks of or the euphoric "intensities" which Jameson, following Lyotard, associates with the fragmented postmodern subject (*Postmodernism* 16). The historical determinism apparent in Zak's biography, also implied in the above-quoted thoughts of Roland Michell about the nature of his own identity, is a denial of the idea that freedom of choice dictates the performances of the postmodern subject.

But, as the example of *Moon Tiger* shows, not all of these novels foreclose on the possibility that some freedom may be exercised by a self lacking an *a priori*, essential definition. Some of the books suggest that, if identity is an effect of history working through language and other sign systems, history itself is also an effect rather than a cause or origin. That is, if it is characteristic of our time that we feel powerless before historical forces, their changing meanings are something that we ourselves produce. Individually, we may, like Zak, lack the capacity to make or master history, but collectively we do construct it in the sense that we determine what it signifies. And if we fabricate history by interpreting human events and processes, then it might not be sophistical to say that in a roundabout way we also construct the subjectivities shaped by that history. This is certainly what Claudia does. Of course, historical interpretations are to some extent constrained by the social contexts in which they occur and by the character of the events to be interpreted. Analogously, self-fashioning is limited and conditioned by factors such as ideology, language, the unconscious, and the environment in which an individual is raised. Some of the novels suggest, though, that these are not so much forces which determine the self, as materials to be transformed by characters who are self-conscious enough to see the possibilities open to them and instinctively flexible enough to improvise upon them.

As Waugh states, this model of identity, closely associated with the work of Nietzsche, is a mutation of a Romantic conception of the self, "an extension of a Coleridgean aesthetic shorn of its secure metaphysical underpinnings" (*Practising Postmodernism* 116). Waugh deserves to be quoted at length on this topic because her formulation illuminates the novels in question:

> Nietzsche talks of the self in terms which post-Kantian criticism has reserved for art. Authentic creation is a suspension of the consciously directed and formulated will in life as well as art. He extends the Romantic concept of the imagination to predict the Freudian sense of the unconscious as a primordially aestheticising mode arising out of body: out of instinct and desire. . . . Here body must be harnessed to a "technology of self" where self-construction displaces self-knowledge. For Foucault, as Nietzsche, human nature is not a hidden essence waiting to be discovered through self-analysis, but an artefact, a sedimented aggregate of those available forms we have chosen to shape into a coherent identity. Otherwise, if we have shunned the responsibility of authentic aesthetic self-creation, we are entirely a fabrication of others. (115)

The emphasis here on an "authentic" self-creation seems more in keeping with post-World War II existentialism than postmodernism. Both movements eschew a belief in an essence which underwrites or structures human identity, but the paradoxical insistence in existentialism that *mauvaise foi* be avoided, that selfhood be authentically enacted through freely chosen, if gratuitous, gestures, is antithetical to Jameson's depiction of the depthless, multiple, "schizophrenic" subject, for whom the idea of authenticity would be meaningless, given that his or her experience of postmodernist culture consists of disconnected moments (*Postmodernism* 27). Existentialism privileges the individual, whereas postmodernism denies the individuality of the subject, or at least deconstructs it.

The treatment of identity by some of the novelists seems closer to the existentialist model outlined here than to Jameson's postmodernist one. The clearest example might be Fowles, who has testified to the influence on his own work of French existentialism (Campbell 466); although he has more recently repudiated its position on freedom as "a wish fulfilment," he still affirms the possibility of achieving "moments or periods of comparative freedom" (Bigsby 117). I have already implied that *A Maggot* downplays the importance of such freedom in stressing the role of history in the formation of ways of thinking about the self, but the novel does in fact hold out the hope that the individual can ultimately resist social determinism. The shadowy aristocrat Bartholomew, like *The French Lieutenant's Woman*'s Sarah Woodruff and Charles Smithson, is a proto-existentialist who has determined to throw off the confining patterns of behaviour dictated by his social class: "I am born with a fixed destiny. . . . I am, as you might be," he says to one of his party on the journey, the actor Lacy, "offered a part in a history, and I am not forgiven for refusing to play it" (37-38). Bartholomew's goal is the exact opposite of that of Zak Rabinovitch, who enacts rather than refuses the roles offered by history.

It is not clear, though, what Bartholomew substitutes for his "fixed destiny." What could comprise a self lacking an essential identity, apart from some variation on or transformation of the patterns of belief and behaviour supplied by society? In refusing to dissipate the uncertainty shrouding Bartholomew's disappearance, Fowles declines to be specific about the nature of the hinted-at metamorphosis of his character. We know that Bartholomew is seeking vitalizing psychological change through an encounter with mysterious forces. We know that he is interested in the religious life of the Celtic druids and that the point of his journey to Stonehenge and to the cavern in Devonshire is to seek spiritual power by enacting rites that have both pagan and Christian elements. But we never learn, unambiguously, what happens to him. Indeed, the novel even fails to answer the basic question of whether the disappearance represents Bartholomew's success or failure in his attempt to transcend history.

There is little doubt, however, that Fowles's intention is to stimulate his readers' imaginations—and thereby to promote their own personal growth—by confronting them with an unsolvable mystery. "Mystery, or unknowing, is energy," writes Fowles in *The Aristos*. "As soon as a mystery is explained, it ceases to be a source of energy" (28). In absconding without warning, like *The Magus*'s Maurice Conchis, Bartholomew acts as Fowles's surrogate as novelist, just as he did before his disappearance by creating various fictional scenarios to be acted out and producing uncertainty about what is real. He performs the equivalent *in* the book of what Fowles does *with* the book in leaving the plot without a denouement and thus inviting readers to become more creatively involved with the text.

The paradox of a mutable self which is both fabricated in performance and yet also authentic or true is explored in *Ever After*. For Bill Unwin, the paradox was embodied in his late wife, the actress Ruth Vaughn, who had the power to incarnate fictional characters so vividly on the stage or screen that their lives seemed more real to the audience than their own. "She was an actress, wasn't she?" thinks Bill. "It was her job: to represent life to people" (131). But who was Ruth herself? Bill protests that, although lacking a solid identity himself (128), he knew the "real" woman behind the performances: "It was *her*, it was *her*, you see, never those roles she dressed in" (83). But when we examine what constituted that core identity, we find that Bill is unable to specify much beyond the naturalness and vivacity that enabled her to be the successful actress that she was (128). Bill's crisis is precipitated by the fact that those special qualities did not survive her death and cannot be revived: "And nothing is left but this impossible absence. This space at your side the size of a woman, the size of a life, the size—of the world" (270). The tragic implication is that, no matter how authentic it seems, an identity lacking an essence or foundational reality is ultimately insubstantial and transient.

The treatment of subjectivity in other novels emphasizes the second rather than the first ingredient in Waugh's recipe, quoted above, of "authentic aesthetic self-creation." *Chatterton*, for example, seems Wildean[1] in its suggestions that identity is simply one of many materials on which the artistic imagination can work to create beautiful artifacts. The novel as a whole thoroughly repudiates the aesthetic credo of sincerity voiced by the Victorian poet Miss Slimmer, who criticizes Wallis's artistic approach to painting Chatterton as "all artifice." "For me," she says, "poetry must be direct and it must be inspired. It will be simple and it will be true" (160). *Chatterton*, however, seems in what it implies about the nature of the self rather to endorse Charles Wychwood's reaction to the discrepant views of Chatterton supplied by the extant biographies:

> In any case, he noticed that each biography described a quite different poet; even the simplest observation by one was contradicted by another, so that nothing seemed certain. He felt that he knew the biographers well, but that he still understood very little about Chatterton. At first Charles had been

---

[1] This adjective seems especially appropriate in view of the fact that one of Ackroyd's novels is *The Last Testament of Oscar Wilde*.

annoyed by these discrepancies but then he was exhilarated by them: for it meant that anything became possible. If there were no truths, everything was true. (127)

Ironically, Chatterton himself, as Ackroyd depicts him, is not deprived of a coherent sense of identity by seeing himself as the product of aesthetic artifice. On the contrary, multiplying himself creatively only confirms for him his essential identity as a genius (92), a "poet born, which is a greater thing than a Gentleman" (87). As Dana Shiller points out ("Redemptive Past" 18), he conceives of his forgeries, not as masks occluding his real self, but as expressions of that self: "I invented my self as a monk of the fifteenth century, Thomas Rowley; I dressed him in Raggs, I made him Blind and then I made him Sing. I compos'd Elegies and Epics, Ballads and Songs, Lyrics and Acrosticks, all of them in that curious contriv'd Style which speedily became the very Token of my own Feelings" (Ackroyd 87).

A similarly varied set of possibilities for self-creation is open to Winterson's character Villanelle. Like Chatterton, she is driven to fabricate personae by a Romantic passion, which marks them as her own and gives her life a teleological direction: "passion is not so much an emotion as a destiny," she says (62). But in *The Passion* the pressure of the historical currents against and with which the self must work is felt more strongly than in *Chatterton*. These currents are identified by Henri, who states that history shunts people into only two categories: "Soldiers and women. That's how the world is. Any other role is temporary. Any other role is a gesture" (45).

To be a woman, in Villanelle's society, is to be diminished and constrained—without, however, being vouchsafed a single, stable sense of identity. What Waugh says about women in our own time certainly applies to those of nineteenth-century Europe, as Winterson presents it. According to Waugh, women and other socially marginalized groups "may *never* have experienced a sense of full subjectivity in the first place. . . . Such Others may, indeed *already* have sensed the extent to which subjectivity is constructed through the institutional dispositions of relations of power, as well as those of fictional convention." As a result, these "Others," Waugh argues, might not find the lessons of postmodernism with regard to identity very startling or disturbing (*Feminine Fictions* 2). Certainly, Villanelle is comfortable with the idea that the self is a fluid, shifting invention. Whereas Henri, as a man in a patriarchal culture, identifies with his role of soldier, Villanelle is able to circumvent the limitations which society would place on her as a woman. Living out her passions involves enacting roles which defy the restrictions of her gender. Disguised as a man, Villanelle asks, "what was myself? Was this breeches and boots self any less real than my garters?" (66).

The objective correlative for the fluidity of her identity is watery, ever-changing Venice, a city which corresponds to the erotic landscapes symbolizing the amorphousness of female identity in the literary criticism of *Possession*'s Leonora Stern (244-46). Byatt may parody the excesses of this sort of feminist criticism, but on the evidence of her novel she seems to be in accord with the notion that identity is a malleable construct that must be actively shaped by the individual if he or she is to be more than the product of historical forces. It is this creative self-fashioning that gives the Victorian poets Ash and LaMotte the inner richness as individuals which is so admired and envied by the novel's modern characters. These scholars seem to assume, mistakenly, that the Victorians—merely by existing before the great age of individualism was destroyed by Freud and other thinkers—were automatically blessed with unshakeably firm self-images. But *Possession* exposes the vulnerability of the Victorian belief in the autonomy of selfhood, suggesting that even then individual identity was not necessarily experienced as solid or monolithic.

Ironically, a rigidly defined sense of self is lacking in Ash himself, the very figure whom Roland, Blackadder, and Cropper expect to compensate, as the subject of their scholarship, for their own lack of inner wholeness. The triumph of Ash's poetic ventriloquism is made possible precisely because, like Keats's ideal poet, he "is the most unpoetical of any thing in existence; because he has no Identity" (Keats 279). "It is difficult to know where to *have* Randolph Ash" (23), reads a sentence that Byatt has imagined the real historical personage Crabb Robinson writing in his famous diary. But this absence of a stable, unchanging identity does not mean that Ash strikes Robinson and his other contemporaries as deprived of selfhood. Rather the dynamism and unceasing curiosity that make Ash a magnetic figure are allied with the creative empathy that enables him to project himself into the various subjects of his dramatic monologues. Like Ackroyd's Chatterton, Ash uses poetry to enlarge and multiply himself. He is enriched by his own unconscious—the source of much of his creativity—whereas the modern characters, following Freud and Lacan, tend to view the unconscious as an alien aspect of the fractured self, not as the creative wellspring of identity.

The novel's modern scholars, then, fail at the task of self-fashioning, and, consequently, they believe themselves to be the helpless pawns of forces beyond their control. As I have mentioned, Roland tends to dismiss his personal identity as a mere illusion; equally influenced by poststructuralism, Maud also questions whether she is anything more than a "matrix for a susurration of texts and codes" (251). As a response to this dilemma, Maud, Roland, and the other twentieth-century academics mistakenly turn to the Victorian writers whom they are studying to supply the self-definition which they themselves lack. This submission has the ironic effect of further diminishing rather than enhancing their inadequate identities. For example, Roland's superior, Professor Blackadder, who is editing the complete works of Ash, finds, disconcertingly, that he has been possessed and negated by his knowledge of the great poet: "There were times when Blackadder allowed himself to see clearly that he would end his working life, that was to say his conscious thinking life, in this task, that all his thoughts would have been another man's thoughts, all his work another man's work" (29). Cropper, too, in "fluently documenting every last item of the days of Randolph Henry Ash . . . had naturally perhaps felt his own identity at times, at the very best of times, as insubstantial, leached into this matter-of-writing, stuff-of-record" (99). Roland, ironically—given his low economic status as a graduate student and his low academic status as Blackadder's underling —feels "superior to Mortimer Cropper, and in some sense equal to Ash, or anyway related to Ash, who had written for him to read intelligently, as best he could" (470).

But Roland's progressive, obsessive immersion in the written record of Ash's thoughts and sentiments does not correspondingly enhance his negligible sense of self. His inner development depends directly on his recognition late in the novel that whatever identity he has is totally separate from Ash's, not contained within it (467). "The pursuit of the letters had distanced him from Ash as they had come closer to Ash's life" (469-70). The "dispossession" of the letter that Roland had stolen from Ash's copy of Vico is preceded by a powerful psychological transformation. He discovers a previously unknown fount of creativity within himself as he feels the seeds of poems that he will write germinate deep in his being (474-75). Formerly believing his subjectivity to be written by codes, he now feels that he has a real identity as a poet, an agent who uses words rather than an illusion who is constituted by them. In this regard, he has obviously become more like Ash by the paradoxical means of distancing himself from the Victorian poet. Jackie Buxton is correct in saying that "Roland . . . becomes the aesthetic, creative heir to Randolph Ash, while Maud remains 'merely' the biological heir to Christabel LaMotte" (216).

Although Roland's metamorphosis is related to his dissociation of himself from Ash, it is, paradoxically, inspired by a reading of one of Ash's books, *The Golden Apples* (471-72). Were this not so, one could easily get the impression that Byatt is linking the development of individual identity with rejection of the past, with a schismatic turning away from history. But what Roland's situation recalls, instead, is Eliot's traditionalism, which involved a readiness to see how the past can be turned to new ends in the present, not a fixation with and slavish imitation of past models. Roland's inspired reading of Ash's poetry leads away from Ash to a vital contemplation of poetic subjects that are entirely Roland's own: "He could hear, or feel, or even almost see, the patterns made by a voice he didn't yet know, but which was his own. The poems were not careful observations, nor yet incantations, nor yet reflections on life and death, though they had elements of all these. . . . He had time to feel the strangeness of before and after; an hour ago there had been no poems, and now they came like rain and were real" (475).

Both his reading of Ash's poetry ("when every word burn[ed] and shin[ed] hard and clear and infinite and exact, like stones of fire, like points of stars in the dark" [471]) and his envisioning of his own poems are characterized by a numinous intensity that marks them as quintessentially Romantic. He abandons poststructuralist thought, reverting to a less vexed conception of subjectivity and authorship in which words have their mysterious origins and grounding in the living presence of individuals. His rejection of sceptical theories of language begins with his compiling "lists of words that resisted arrangement into the sentences of literary criticism or theory" (431). This leads to his assertion that some signifiers are concretely attached to signifieds:

> He had been taught that language was essentially inadequate, that it could never speak what was there, that it only spoke itself.
> He thought about [Ash's] death mask. He could and could not say that the mask and the man were dead. What had happened to him was that the ways in which it *could* be said had become more interesting than the idea that it could not. (473)

Roland's conversion to a belief that language has an integral connection to both the self and the world has important implications regarding the status of the imagination. His transformation rests tacitly on a Coleridgean belief that the imagination has transcendent power as a tool of perception. The difficulty is that *Possession* has already planted in its readers the idea that the imagination, like personal identity, is an intertextual construct, the contingent product of narrative and other cultural systems. Roland's altered views, never justified in rational terms, are the result of the very sort of emotional or existential experience that critical theory has conditioned him, and us, to dismiss as insubstantial. What results from this conflict is ambiguity. This same ambiguity arises from the treatment of the imagination in the other principal novels discussed in my study. It will be a central theme in the ensuing, final chapter.

CHAPTER FIVE

The Historical Imagination

As novels rather than actual histories, the eight works considered in this book obviously go well beyond the historical archive to incorporate invented characters and situations. In a novel such as *The Passion*, which is notable for its magic realism, many of the events even lack verisimilitude. But I would argue that even when they abandon plausibility the novels paradoxically assert their affinity with, rather than their difference from, historical writing, which is also dependent upon imaginative activity. Faced with the need to construct a coherent historical narrative out of the available evidence, the historian necessarily must, according to Collingwood, rely upon his or her imagination: "the historian's picture of the past is . . . in every detail an imaginary picture, and its necessity is at every point the necessity of the *a priori* imagination" (245). Collingwood holds that the historian begins with an imaginative construction, which is primary, and then assesses the evidence in relation to it: "So far from relying for its validity upon the support of given facts, [the historian's imaginative fabrication] actually serves as the touchstone by which we decide whether alleged facts are genuine" (244). The basis of historical activity, in this view, is thus not a reality to which historiography can be proved unequivocally to correspond but a hypothetical construction. "The imaginary, simply as such," Collingwood says, "is neither unreal nor real" (241).

Collingwood's view is dated to the extent that he locates the source of imaginative activity in the exclusively private consciousness of the individual historian rather than in the broadly cultural and political sphere. Nevertheless, his ideas are a challenge to traditionally empiricist notions of the writing of history. According to White, good historians have rarely been bound wholly by such notions, since they have been sensitive to "the purely provisional nature of [their] characterizations of events, agents, and agencies found in the always incomplete historical record." But he adds that "in general there has been a reluctance to consider historical narratives as what they most manifestly are: verbal fictions, the contents of which are as much *invented* as *found* and the forms of which have more in common with their counterparts in literature than they have with those in the sciences" (*Tropics* 82). Disputing that history can actually attain the status of a science (43), White adds that "we should no longer naively expect that statements about a given epoch or complex of events in the past 'correspond' to some preexistent body of 'raw facts' " (47). Two of the barriers to history's becoming rigorously scientific are exposed by Robert Holton, who notes that the incomplete nature of historical data and the restricted cultural contexts within which the historians themselves live and work inevitably make historiography less than fully accurate and comprehensive (6).

The novels considered here reflect self-consciously upon, and thus bring to the fore, the ambiguous character of attempts to know the past; all are metafictions which interrogate the ontological status of their own historical representations. In their self-probing, self-critical qualities, all eight are novels of the kind that LaCapra champions as models for historical writing (132). As I have shown, the books feature characters who are surrogates for their authors as aspiring historians of one kind or another. Most of the protagonists are also creative artists who traffic in fabrication and artifice, and accordingly they focus our attention on the link between fiction and history. The most provocative formulation of this equation is the already-quoted remark of Ackroyd's eccentric novelist Harriet Slope: history is "the one thing we have to make up for ourselves" (226). The narrator of Barnes's self-reflexive meditation "Parenthesis" expatiates on a similar notion:

> History isn't what happened. History is just what historians tell us. There was a pattern, a plan, a movement, expansion, the march of democracy; it is a tapestry, a flow of events, a complex narrative, connected, explicable. One good story leads to another. . . . The history of the world? Just voices echoing in the dark; images that burn for a few centuries and then fade; stories, old stories that sometimes seem to overlap. . . . We make up a story to cover the facts we don't know or can't accept; we keep a few true facts and spin a new story around them. Our panic and our pain are only eased by soothing fabulation; we call it history.   (240)

That Barnes's narrator does not conceive of history as dispensing altogether with facts corroborates the point I made in Chapter Two that the construction of history, as the novels dramatize it, is not a free activity. And yet, the term "fabulation" and the quoted passage as a whole deny that the facts anchor or ground historical narratives to any significant extent. Barnes's statement recalls the reference of Lively's Claudia to "the confection of fact and fantasy that is how we know the world" (62).

Also undermining an objectivist view of the historical enterprise is the derived, dependent character of "facts." The philosopher F. H. Bradley and the historian Carl Becker many years ago acknowledged that what will be construed as fact depends upon historically mutable conceptual schemes (Holton 13; Martin 325). Martin quotes a magazine article of 1910 in which Becker said that "it is 'almost impossible to distinguish [fact] from theory, to which it is commonly supposed to be so completely antithetical'" (325). All eight of the novels share this kind of sophistication about the limits of the empirical method of gaining knowledge of the past, but none rejects the method entirely. Their ambivalence is in keeping with Hutcheon's contention that "[i]n both fiction and history writing today, our confidence in empiricist and positivist epistemologies has been shaken—shaken, but perhaps not yet destroyed" (*Poetics* 106).

The distrust of the empirical approach to history is shown in *A Maggot* through Fowles's treatment of the lawyer Ayscough, whose total acceptance of the monistic logic of science is shown to rob him of generosity and tolerance, and to make him blind to the multifaceted, complex character of experience. His method is shown to be inadequate to clear up the uncertainty surrounding Bartholomew's disappearance from the cave in Devon. Ayscough's closed-mindedness and tendency to objectify and bully witnesses could be read as a dramatization of Fowles's belief that science is a "reifying and self-imprisoning" system (*Enigma* 125). One could argue that Fowles unfairly characterizes science, since its practitioners must be open, not closed, to the possibility that evidence gained through experimentation might disprove their hypotheses. But I think that what he is objecting to is the widespread assumption that *only* the scientific method can lead to genuine knowledge. What Fowles wants to show is not that science, with all of its obvious successes, has no place in life but that other ways of knowing, such as the artistic and visionary one personified by Lee, are superior in important respects. The latter orientation, for Fowles, is more in tune with the mystery and hazard and ongoingness of existence.

But it would be misleading to suggest that the imaginative or artistic mode, as it is figured in *A Maggot* and the other novels, is in all respects separate from and opposed to the empirical one. It is well known that some important scientific discoveries have been made possible by imaginative, highly metaphoric leaps of thought, and it has even been argued that "many, if not most scientific interpretations are inherently a matter of thinking by metaphor and analogy" (O'Kell 194). It is equally true that artistic activity has an empirical component in that it bears, with varying degrees of directness, on people's "first-hand" experiences, however mediated by cultural codes those experiences may be. If historical representations are imaginative constructions, these patternings incorporate and make sense of real happenings, or at least of previous accounts of them. The most accurate way to describe the relationship in the novels between the empirical and the imaginative in relation to history might be to say that the former is subsumed within the latter. As White argues, "we can only know the *actual* by contrasting it with or likening it to the *imaginable*" (*Tropics* 98). It seems unlikely, therefore, that the actual could ever finally be disentangled from the imaginable. Perhaps this is why writers such as Barnes, whose *History of the World* puts biblical figures such as Noah on an even ontological footing with people drawn from the historical archive, mix myth and history in such an inextricable fashion.

One corollary of these thoughts about the centrality of the imagination is that historical activity, while not without constraints, is endless, since the archive can always be reconfigured imaginatively. As Collingwood says, each "present has a past of its own, and any imaginative reconstruction of the past aims at reconstructing the past of the present, the present in which the act of imagination is going on" (247). All of the novels register suspicion of methods of historical scholarship which treat the past as something finite and concrete, as something which can be collected and possessed and known completely. The young academics in *Possession* make this mistake when they hoard the letters written by the Victorian poets Randolph Ash and Christabel LaMotte. In ignoring their own role in fabricating the narrative of the love affair between Ash and LaMotte, Roland and Maud are guilty, in LaCapra's terms, of making a fetish of the archive, treating it as though it contained the past in its entirety (92).[1] Ash's biographer Mortimer Cropper more literally fetishizes the nineteenth-century material objects owned by or associated with the poet. He seems to believe that Ash somehow lives on in these items.

But Byatt's unflattering presentation of Cropper, like that of Ayscough by Fowles, is an invitation to view his reification of the past as

---

[1] "The archive as a fetish," LaCapra asserts, "is a literal substitute for the 'reality' of the past which is 'always already' lost for the historian. When it is fetishized, the archive is more than the repository of traces of the past which may be used in its inferential reconstruction. It is a stand-in for the past that brings the mystified experience of the thing itself—an experience that is always open to question when one deals with writing or other inscriptions" (92).

deathly. The past cannot be frozen because, in a sense, it remains vitally unfinished as long as we continue to enter into ever-new Bakhtinian dialogues with the texts that comprise the historical record. "Why should historical research not . . . remain incomplete, existing as a possibility and not fading into knowledge?" thinks Ackroyd's Philip Slack (213). Of course, in a literal, narrow sense the research is completed when Slack discovers the fraudulent character of his friend's Chatterton documents, but, as Dana Shiller rightly notes of both *Chatterton* and *Possession,* this knowledge strikes readers as of secondary importance: "This notion of a history richer in possibilities than it is in empirical facts permeates both *Chatterton* and *Possession*: both novels do, in the end, offer explanations, but in both cases these seem less important than the spirit of curiosity which gives rise to them, and both sets of explanations seem themselves provisional when contrasted with what, in the novels, is shown to be unknowable" ("Neo-Victorian" 11).

If at times the various novels considered here celebrate the incompleteness and openness of history as possibility rather than as certainty, at other points they express anxiety about the epistemological validity of the historical imagination. There is, for example, more than a little ambiguity in the refrain of both narrators of *The Passion*: "I'm telling you stories. Trust me" (5, 13, 40, 69, 160). While the protagonists of Winterson, Fowles, and Ackroyd glorify the power of imagination, the writers themselves, in company with the other novelists, are of course aware that the metaphysical basis for Romanticism's exaltation of this faculty has been radically undermined since the early nineteenth century. All are sensitive to the ways in which the imagination has been demystified and deconstructed in our own time. The decentering of the subject discussed in the preceding chapter dovetails with poststructuralist thought about the death of the author as the creative force behind the text: just as the individual is no longer presumed to be a coherent, meaning-generating center, so the author's creative power is no longer credited as the origin of literature and other forms of writing.

In *Possession* the failure of confidence in historical representations lacking unequivocal status as objective reality is located not only in our own time but also in the nineteenth century. "It is often seen as a modern discovery that history is necessarily fictive," writes Byatt in an essay on Browning; "it was in fact a pervasive nineteenth century perception" (*Passions of the Mind* 35). In such a context it is hardly surprising that Byatt's poet Ash (who has obviously been modelled principally on Browning) does not have unbridled trust in the even more explicitly fabricated products of his own "historical imagination" (25): "[I]f I construct a fictive eye-witness account—a credible plausible account—am I lending life to truth with my fiction—or verisimilitude to a colossal Lie with my feverish imagination?" (168). Although there is no simple answer to this question, he does manage to sustain a more buoyant, optimistic posture than do the twentieth-century protagonists. Romanticism has not yet been wholly discredited for him, as it will be for many of those who succeed him. As the following contrast between Coleridge and Browning suggests, Byatt conceives of the Victorians as occupying an intermediate position between ours and that of the first-generation English Romantics: "It is a truism that the Romantic poet came to see his own inspiration and creation as divine, poetry, as spilt religion, his work, as Coleridge said, an echo in the finite mind of the infinite I AM. Browning makes no such high claims—he calls his work '—Mimic creation, galvanism for life, / But still a glory portioned in the scale'" (*Passions of the Mind* 47).

However glorious "Mimic creation" might seem, it is but a short step away from "fabulation," "forgery," "plagiarism," and "propaganda," which are some of the words used by Barnes, Ackroyd, and Williams in order to point up the dubious character of attempts to represent the past. These terms take on a more generalized, metaphoric expansion of meaning, so that they come to designate not only instances of fraudulent communication but also honest—though inevitably flawed—attempts to tell the truth about the past. After cataloguing the numerous instances in Ackroyd's novel of plagiarism and forgery in literature and painting, Hutcheon properly concludes that *Chatterton* "is a novel self-consciously, even excessively, *about* representation—its illusions and its powers, its possibilities and its politics" (*Politics* 96). In *Star Turn* it is Amos Barking's wartime job as a propagandist for the British that directs attention to how attempts to convey the reality of past experiences are distorted by ideology. He boasts that he "can make one German plane downed over the Channel sound like the end of the line for the Reich," but he then adds, "I am determined not to write propaganda for myself. I am going to rise above what I have become, transform myself into a truth teller" (17). Amos has already confessed, however, that his task is bedeviled not only by his penchant for lying but also by the fallibility of his memory and imagination. Doubt "infects all my memory," he tells us. "I sometimes think I dreamed Isaac. Even Isaac, the most important person in my life" (15).

The dilemma posed by the ambiguous status of the imagination becomes acute when we reflect on what is at stake in historical activity as it is dramatized in most of the novels. As I argued in Chapter One and

Chapter Two, by trying to establish continuity with past eras and long-dead individuals, the novels' characters are trying to imbue their own lives with the values associated with those times and people. Some of the characters are attempting even more: to "resurrect" the dead by empathizing with them imaginatively and lending them their voices. This is what Byatt's Ash hopes to achieve with his poetic ventriloquism (104, 168), and it is also the motive for Swift's protagonist's researches into the life of Matthew Pearce (97), whose resuscitation is meant to compensate for the loss of Unwin's wife. Ackroyd's Wychwood, too, by seeking through his historical activity to overturn the story of Chatterton's early suicide, is trying to free the poet from the clutches of death, just as Henry Wallis had in the nineteenth century by painting the poet on his deathbed. "You *are* a Resurrectionist, Henry. You can bring the dead to life, I see," says Meredith, Wallis's model, upon seeing the portrait (156). Ironically, Chatterton's forgeries, as Ackroyd accounts for them, are intended to produce a similar result; Chatterton says of the medieval manuscripts which were his inspiration, "I decided to shore up these ancient Fragments with my own Genius: thus the Living and the Dead were to be reunited" (85).

A fear shared by these authors is that the exercise of the historical imagination might have the unintended, perverse effect of casting a deathly pall over the living, rather than resurrecting the dead. Perhaps such an uncertainty is behind LaCapra's not-fully-explained reference to "the strangeness of a dialogue with the dead who are reconstructed through their 'textualized' remainders" (36). In any event, this worry is quite explicit in *Chatterton*. Ackroyd's readers cannot overlook the fact that what Wallis the "Resurrectionist" has brought back to "life" in his painting is Chatterton's corpse. This fact ironically undercuts Wallis's feeling that "[n]either he nor Chatterton could now wholly die" (170). In fact, the novel might well have been titled *The Death of Chatterton*, and not only because it concludes with an image of the poet's dead body sprawled across the bed in his tiny garret room. The narration of Chatterton's death, lengthy and detailed, is broken into several parts and interspersed with other scenes. The effect—the suggestion that his dying is protracted throughout the novel—is reinforced overtly in the following description of one of Charles Wychwood's poems: "he had been trying to describe how time is nothing other than the pattern of deaths which succeed one another" (169). But Wychwood's own death does not so much succeed Chatterton's as replicate it and merge with it.

It is true that there is an intimation of spiritual transcendence in Chatterton's vision, at the moment of his death, of Wychwood and

Meredith standing beside him. "I will live forever, he tells them. They link hands and bow towards the sun" (234). But there is surely something paradoxical in that what Ackroyd has emphasized in his management of the narrative is not so much the sense of rebirth from death as the perpetuation of death. After all, Charles's hypothesis that Chatterton escaped its clutches by faking suicide is proved false. It could be said that, instead of rescuing his eighteenth-century predecessor from death, Charles only succeeds in following him into it. This is not the opinion of his widow Vivien, however, or of his friend Philip, who asserts that "[t]he important thing is what Charles imagined, and we can keep hold of that. That isn't an illusion. The imagination never dies" (232). But this optimism is based on faith alone, and by incorporating a dissenting point of view into his novel Ackroyd reminds us that it is equally possible to doubt the truth and permanence of the products of the imagination. In response to Charles's claim that poetry survives, Andrew Flint angrily exclaims, "Don't you realize . . . that nothing survives now? Everything is instantly forgotten. . . . There are no standards to encourage permanence—only novelty, and the whole endless cycle of new objects. And books are simply objects. . . . And poetry is no different. Poetry is disposable, too. . . . Yes, [books] survive. But don't you realize it's just another kind of death? Five hundred books of poetry published in any one year—they're piled up in the library stacks, or they gather dust on the shelves. . . . A monument to human ambition and human indifference" (150).

Possession also insinuates that the endeavour to resurrect and give voice to the dead may result merely in a trafficking with the dead that is itself a kind of death. "You have this thing about this dead man," Val says to Roland. "Who had a thing about dead people" (19). This accusation is supported by the novel's symbolism. The narrator explicitly refers to the "Ash factory" in the basement of the British Museum as the "Inferno," in contradistinction to the "Paradiso" of the Reading Room above with its splendid dome (26). The significance of Roland and Val's dank and dreary basement flat in this connection is obvious: Roland is symbolically interred with the dead, shut out by his landlady from the garden of fulfillment outside his door. Cropper's robbing of Ash's grave is also germane in relation to this symbolism of death. This act, the novel implies, discloses the true significance of his obsession with the material objects owned by Ash. Cropper seems to believe that Ash somehow lives on in these items, or at least that they constitute a metonymic path that will lead him to that enduring, originary presence. He does discover the letter buried by Ash's wife, Ellen, but the trail finally ends at Ash's lifeless corpse. Buxton is probably right to say that at bottom his interest in the dead poet is "necrophiliac and ghoulish" (206).

It is obvious that the exercise of the historical imagination in these novels carries with it great risks and rewards. The aim goes beyond the desire to establish continuity with the past or to impose order upon it. The goal is to transcend time altogether and to overcome death, to supply immortality. And owing to the equation made by the novels between historical representation and imaginative literature, the immortality which they seek is essentially that which has traditionally been claimed for great art. Just as Barnes's narrator in "Shipwreck" sings Géricault's praises for transforming a historical catastrophe into an enduring work of art, just as Chatterton and Wychwood extol the permanent character of poetry, so Swift's Bill Unwin justifies literature as "verbal eternity" (27). His own historical project is of this same order in being intended to free Matthew (and, by extension, Bill himself) from the obliterating sweep of time and change. Bill certainly views the journal which Matthew kept in just this way, as a "small plea, after all, for non-extinction. A life, after all, beyond life" (221). "O death-defiers of this world!" Bill exclaims. "O luminaries, O immortalists! To leave one's mark! To build a bridge, christen a theory, name a pear, write a book. The struggle for existence? Ha! The struggle for *remembrance*" (245).

Fowles, who has said quite directly that "art best conquers time" (*Aristos* 184), manifests a desire to achieve this goal in *A Maggot*, as does his character Bartholomew, who is fascinated by Stonehenge because he believes that its builders "had pierced some part of the mystery of time" (144). Stonehenge, according to Fowles, overwhelms visitors with "the presentness of its past" (*Enigma* 51) and manifests "an obsession with defying time and death" (*Enigma* 18). What he would like *A Maggot* to do, by incarnating the same sense of mystery apparent at Stonehenge, is to abolish history, to remove the two-hundred-and-fifty-year gap between his characters and his readers and to institute an eternal world, that "hugely extended now" which he claims artists and mystics have the capacity to inhabit (*Maggot* 426). This accomplishment, Fowles believes, would require the full imaginative involvement of both author and readers, which in turn would depend upon what Fowles calls "the inmost characteristic of art—mystery. For what good science tries to eliminate, good art seeks to provoke—mystery, which is lethal to the one and vital to the other" (*Aristos* 153). "Choosing not to know," he says, "in an increasingly 'known,' structured, ordained, predictable world, becomes almost a freedom, a last refuge of the self" (*Enigma* 125). Accordingly, Fowles envelopes his eighteenth-century subject matter in a haze of uncertainty in the hope of gaining the freshness and immediacy of "that weird tense grammar does not allow, the imaginary present" (*Maggot* 386).

The impediment to achieving this timeless present is historical knowledge, without which, ironically enough, the creation of a "historiographic metafiction" such as *A Maggot* would be impossible. Too much uncertainty and mystery would obviously be incompatible with the goal of creating a verisimilitudinous picture of eighteenth-century life. Fowles is, of course, aware of this conundrum. Knowledge is inescapable, as his character Bartholomew is only too aware, despite his aspirations. As the actor Lacy testifies, the aristocrat contrasted the wise unknowing of the builders of Stonehenge with the constraining awareness of people of his own era: "They knew they knew nothing. . . . We moderns are corrupted by our past, our learning, our historians . . ." (144). How can one choose not to know, in other words, when one already does know? What follows from Bartholomew's train of thought is that it is not wholly possible to obliterate the past or avoid being conditioned by it. The narrator of *A Maggot* expresses the matter succinctly when he says that most of us are "equal victims in the debtors' prison of history, and equally unable to leave it" (231).

Swift's novel also betrays an awareness that the historical imagination cannot ultimately defeat time. The unequal contest is symbolized in *Ever After* in the clock, made by Matthew Pearce's father and inherited by Bill as a wedding present, on which is inscribed the Virgilian motto *Amor Vincit Omnia*. Love and imagination, linked in the novel in being the two kinds of experience through which Bill tries to overcome the limits of mortality, have, of course, traditionally been identified with each other, an association justified in down-to-earth terms by Barnes's narrator in "Parenthesis": "You can't love someone without imaginative sympathy, without beginning to see the world from another point of view" (241). Bill acknowledges that love cannot conquer time, quoting the following lines of Raleigh: "*Even such is time, which takes in trust / Our youth, our joys, and all we have, / And pays us but with age and dust*" (77).

Despite being passed down in Bill's family for a century or so, the clock does not represent a historical continuum protected from the ravages of change. The novel questions whether, even within the relatively brief span of one hundred years, historical differences between individuals and cultures can be so easily overcome. Can people be significantly connected to their predecessors in the absence of a shared conception of time as an environment in which a purposeful design involving humanity can be played out? Such a conception was no longer available to Matthew after his crisis of faith, but it had been to his father, who, to Matthew as a child (at least as Bill imagines him), seemed "to be engaged not only in the making of clocks but in the manufacture of this vital stuff called Time, this stuff which Matthew still thought of as being essentially human in meaning, the companion and guardian of human affairs" (115). If there is no Time with a capital *T*, no transcendent History, can the histories which we devise knit our lives together into patterns that are other than contingent and inherently pointless?

Bill certainly fears that a fundamental historical discontinuity destabilizes the bridges which we erect over the gap separating the present from the past. I use the metaphor of bridges deliberately, for Swift employs it in the novel to suggest that history is schismatic. Bill makes the following remarks about the Tamar railroad bridge designed by I. K. Brunel, the real historical figure whom Swift works into the narrative by making the fictional Matthew his assistant:

> To build a bridge! To span a void! And what voids, what voids there were. He would never know. Need never know. . . . He was safe. . . . Safe within the limits of an old, safe world. Only seven months after his bridge was opened and only two months after his death, Darwin would publish . . . his *Origin of Species*. (217)

The point to be inferred here is that, while the material bridge still exists, the world which it would attach to the future has vanished owing to revolutionary changes in knowledge, not least of which was that effected by Darwin. The modern world which he ushered in, Bill implies, was not safe, but his emphasis on Brunel's own safety is surely ironic in view of Bill's awareness that the famous engineer would cross his bridge only when terminally ill, "pulled slowly, as if on a hearse" (217). How can historical reconstruction, Swift seems to be asking rhetorically, possibly span the unbridgeable gulf of death?

Swift, in company with the other novelists, is aware of the contradiction involved in using the historical novel—which by definition sensitizes us to the chronological medium in which human events occur—to oppose the march of time. If by means of the historical imagination the writer attempts to project his or her mind into human events as they unfold in time, then how can that imagination transcend history? How can its exercise be redemptive if the effect is to plunge us back into the flow of time, change, decay, and death rather than to lift us above it? This dilemma is broached overtly in *Ever After* when Unwin narrates how as a child he assembled a scale model, given to him as a present by his stepfather, Sam Ellison, of the fighter plane in which Sam's brother was killed during World War II. Ellison clearly views the building of the model as a commemoration of his brother's sacrifice and as a symbolic reversal of the destruction which took his life. But young Bill's fastidious, authentic bit of historical reconstruction does not end when the parts have been painted and glued together. He next sets fire to the model, and, after he throws it from his upstairs window, the plane crashes on the lawn near his horrified stepfather, whom he bitterly resents (73-74). In this paradigmatic action the representation of history becomes, not a way of denying or compensating for its ravages, but a reenactment of them. The representation of history becomes a part of history, not a refuge from it.

Barnes's "Upstream!" contains a narrative development which illustrates the same phenomenon, or one very like it. During the filming of a movie closely based upon historical accounts of a journey by raft up a South American river undertaken during the eighteenth century by two Jesuit priests, one of the two leading actors is killed during the rehearsal of a scene in which one is supposed to save the other from drowning after the raft capsizes. The attempt to "turn catastrophe into art" (125) becomes just another of history's fatal catastrophes, just as the endeavour to understand and communicate the patterns and meanings of history is engulfed by the violence of history in "The Visitors," when Franklin Hughes, who is employed to give historical lectures on a cruise ship, is forced at gunpoint by Arab terrorists to give the passengers a historical justification of their intention to execute two of them every hour until the terrorists' demands have been met. Hughes does as he is told, improvising an anti-Israeli, pro-Arab lecture on the history of the Middle East in which he tells the captives, "We, alas, are not civilians. The Zionists have made this happen" (56). Numerous members of his audience are subsequently slaughtered before the terrorists are overcome by the American Special Forces.

What narrative situations such as those described above signify is the strict limits of the power of the historical imagination. Attempts to achieve continuity with a desired past or to discover coherence in a threateningly disordered one are frustrated by the mutability of the historical process. No link with or pattern projected onto the past can be frozen; all will be dissolved in the ongoing flux of time. None of the novels discussed here invites us to aver, as Avrom Fleishman could in 1971, that historical fiction has the power "to lift the contemplation of the past above both the present and the past, to see it in its universal character, freed of the urgency of historical engagement" (14).

What the novels do attempt, in full awareness of the forces at work against such an endeavour, is to establish continuity with and make sense of the past. That the successes are tenuous and ephemeral does not negate them entirely. In this book, I have shown the ways in which the mediated character of the historical enterprise renders it problematic, but the novels also remind us that mediation is what prevents schism from occurring, what enables the connection between the present and the past to be made at all. Viewed in this light, the novels' postmodern self-consiousness does not so much render their historical representations insubstantial as reveal what makes it possible to create them.

WORKS CITED

Ackroyd, Peter. *Chatterton*. 1987. London: Abacus-Sphere, 1988.

———. *Hawksmoor*. 1985. London: Abacus-Sphere, 1986.

Alter, Robert. *Partial Magic: The Novel as a Self-Conscious Genre*. Berkley: U of California P, 1975.

———. *The Pleasures of Reading in an Ideological Age*. New York: Simon and Schuster, 1989.

Bakhtin, Mikhail. *The Dialogic Imagination: Four Essays*. Trans. Caryl Emerson and Michael Holquist. Austin: U of Texas P, 1981.

Barnes, Julian. *A History of the World in 10 1/2 Chapters*. New York: Knopf, 1989.

Barthes, Roland. "To Write: An Intransitive Verb?" Trans. Gerald Kamber and Bernard Vannier. *The Structuralist Controversy: The Languages of Criticism and the Sciences of Man*. 1970. Ed. Richard Macksey and Eugenio Donato. Baltimore: Johns Hopkins UP, 1972. 134-45.

Becker, Carl L. *The Heavenly City of the Eighteenth-Century Philosophers*. New Haven: Yale UP, 1932.

Bennett, Tony. *Outside Literature*. London: Routledge, 1990.

Bigsby, Christopher, and Heide Ziegler. "John Fowles." *The Radical Imagination and the Liberal Tradition: Interviews with Contemporary English and American Novelists*. London: Junction: 1982.

Booth, Wayne C. *The Company We Keep: An Ethics of Fiction*. Berkley: U of California P, 1988.

Bradbury, Malcolm. *Possibilities: Essays on the State of the Novel*. Oxford: Oxford UP, 1973.

Brookner, Anita. "Eminent Victorians and Others." *Spectator* 3 Mar. 1990: 35.

Brooks, Peter. *Reading for the Plot: Design and Intention in Narrative*. 1984. New York: Vintage-Random, 1985.

Buxton, Jackie. "What's Love Got to Do with It? Postmodernism and *Possession*." *English Studies in Canada* 22 (1996): 199-219.

Byatt, A. S. *Passions of the Mind: Selected Writings*. London: Chatto, 1991.

———. *Possession: A Romance*. London: Vintage, 1990.

Campbell, James. "An Interview with John Fowles." *Contemporary Literature* 17 (1976): 455-69.

Chatman, Seymour. *Story and Discourse: Narrative Structure in Fiction and Film.* Ithaca: Cornell UP, 1978.

Collingwood, R. G. *The Idea of History.* Rev. ed. 1993. Ed. Jan Van Der Dussen. Oxford: Oxford UP, 1994.

Connor, Steven. *Postmodernist Culture: An Introduction to Theories of the Contemporary.* Oxford: Blackwell, 1989.

Daiches, David. *The Novel and the Modern World.* Rev. ed. Chicago: Phoenix-U of Chicago P, 1960.

D'Amico, Robert. *Historicism and Knowledge.* London: Routledge, 1989.

Eagleton, Terry. *Literary Theory: An Introduction.* Minneapolis: U of Minnesota P, 1983.

———. *The Ideology of the Aesthetic.* Oxford: Blackwell, 1990.

Easthope, Antony. "Eliot, Pound, and the Subject of Postmodernism." *After the Future: Postmodern Times and Places.* Ed. Gary Shapiro. Albany: State U of New York P, 1990. 53-66.

Edgar, David. "Prostitute's Apocalypse." *Listener* 7 Nov. 1985: 29-30.

Eliot, T. S. *Selected Prose of T. S. Eliot.* Ed. Frank Kermode. New York: Harcourt, 1975.

Essex, David. "Review of John Fowles's *A Maggot*: The Novel as Koan." *Eighteenth-Century Life* 10.1 (1986): 80-81.

Finney, Brian. "Peter Ackroyd, Postmodernist Play, and *Chattterton*." *Twentieth-Century Literature* 38 (1992): 240-61.

Fish, Stanley. *Is There a Text in This Class? The Authority of Interpretive Communities.* Cambridge: Harvard UP, 1980.

Fleishman, Avrom. *The English Historical Novel: Walter Scott to Virginia Woolf.* Baltimore: Johns Hopkins UP, 1971.

Fowles, John. *The Aristos.* Rev. ed. New York: Plume-New American Library, 1970.

———. *A Maggot.* Toronto: Collins, 1985.

———. *The French Lieutenant's Woman.* New York: Signet, 1969.

Fowles, John and Barry Brukoff. *The Enigma of Stonehenge.* London: Cape, 1980.

Fowles, John, and Daniel Halpern. "A Sort of Exile in Lyme Regis." *London Magazine* Mar. 1971: 34-46.

Frank, Joseph. *The Idea of Spatial Form.* New Brunswick: Rutgers UP, 1991.

Gąsiorek, Andrzej. *Post-War British Fiction: Realism and After.* London: Arnold, 1995.

Graff, Gerald. *Literature against Itself: Literary Ideas in Modern Society.* Chicago: U of Chicago P, 1979.

Holton, Robert. *Jarring Witnesses: Modern Fiction and the Representation of History.* New York: Harvester Wheatsheaf, 1994.

Hutcheon, Linda. *A Poetics of Postmodernism: History, Theory, Fiction.* London: Routledge, 1988.

————. *The Politics of Postmodernism.* New Accents. London: Routledge, 1989.

Jameson, Fredric. *Postmodernism, or, the Cultural Logic of Late Capitalism.* Durham: Duke UP, 1991.

————. *The Political Unconscious: Narrative as a Socially Symbolic Act.* Ithaca: Cornell UP, 1981.

Jenkyns, Richard. "Disinterring Buried Lives." *Times Literary Supplement* 2-8 Mar. 1990: 213-14.

Keats, John. "To Richard Woodhouse." 27 Oct. 1818. *John Keats: Selected Poems and Letters.* Ed. Douglas Bush. Boston: Houghton, 1959. 279-80.

Kermode, Frank. *The Sense of an Ending: Studies in the Theory of Fiction.* Oxford: Oxford UP, 1966.

LaCapra, Dominick. *History and Criticism.* Ithaca: Cornell UP, 1985.

Lee, Alison. *Realism and Power: Postmodern British Fiction.* London: Routledge, 1990.

Leitch, Vincent B. *Cultural Criticism, Literary Theory, Poststructuralism.* New York: Columbia UP, 1992.

Lerner, Laurence. "Against Historicism." *New Literary History* 24 (1993): 273-92.

Liu, Alan. "Local Transcendence: Cultural Criticism, Postmodernism, and the Romanticism of Detail." *Representations* 32 (1990): 75-113.

Lively, Penelope. *Moon Tiger.* 1987. London: Penguin, 1988.

Lodge, David. *Working with Structuralism: Essays and Reviews on Nineteenth- and Twentieth-Century Literature.* 1981. London: Ark-Routledge, 1986.

Lyotard, Jean-François. "Answering the Question: What Is Postmodernism?" Trans. Regis Durand. Lyotard 71-82.

Lyotard. Jean-François. *The Postmodern Condition: A Report on Knowledge.* Trans. Geoff Bennington and Brian Massumi. Theory and History of Literature, vol. 10. Minneapolis: U of Minnesota P, 1984.

McHale, Brian. *Postmodernist Fiction.* London: Methuen, 1987.

Martin, Raymond. "Forum: Raymond Martin, Joan W. Scott, and Ushing Strout on *Telling the Truth about History.*" *History and Theory* 34 (1995): 320-29.

Miller, J. Hillis. "Narrative and History." *English Literary History* 41 (1974): 455-73.

Miller, Walter, Jr. "*A Maggot.*" *New York Times Book Review* 8 Sept. 1985: 11.

Mink, Louis. *Historical Understanding.* Ed. Brian Fay, Eugene O. Golob, and Richard T. Vann. Ithaca: Cornell UP, 1987.

Montrose, Louis. "Professing the Renaissance: The Poetics and Politics of Culture." *The New Historicism.* Ed. H. Aram Veeser. New York: Routledge, 1989. 15-36.

Moran, Mary Hurley. "Penelope Lively's *Moon Tiger*: A Feminist 'History of the World.'" *Frontiers* 11 (1990): 89-95.

O'Kell, Robert. "Science, Culture, and 'Discourse': Education for the Twenty-first Century." *Physics in Canada* 47 (1991): 190-95.

89

Pease, Donald E. "Author." *Critical Terms for Literary Study*. Ed. Frank Lentricchia and Thomas McLaughlin. Chicago: U of Chicago P, 1990. 105-17.

Perkins, David. *A History of Modern Poetry: From the 1890s to the High Modernist Mode*. Cambridge: Belknap, 1976. vol. 1.

————. *Is Literary History Possible?* Baltimore: Johns Hopkins UP, 1992.

Pinter, Harold. *The Homecoming*. 1965. London: Methuen, 1966.

Poirier, Richard. *The Performing Self: Compositions and Decompositions in the Languages of Contemporary Life*. New York: Oxford UP, 1971.

Sage, Lorna. "Unwin Situation." *Times Literary Supplement* 21 Feb. 1992: 6.

Shiller, Dana. "Neo-Victorian Literature: Reinventing the Past." Unpublished essay presented at the Twentieth-Century Literature Conference, University of Louisville, Feb. 1994.

————. "The Redemptive Past in the Neo-Victorian Novel." Unpublished essay forthcoming in *Studies in the Novel*.

Shilling, Jane. "On a Fine Romance." *Punch* 23 Mar. 1990: 41.

Spanos, William V. *Repetitions: The Postmodern Occasion in Literature and Culture*. Baton Rouge: Louisiana State UP, 1987.

Swift, Graham. *Ever After*. 1992. New York: Vintage, 1993.

Todorov, Tzvetan. *The Poetics of Prose*. Trans. Richard Howard. Ithaca: Cornell UP, 1977.

Updike, John. *Hugging the Shore: Essays and Criticism*. New York: Knopf, 1983.

Waugh, Patricia. *Feminine Fictions: Revisiting the Postmodern*. London: Routledge, 1989.

————. *Metafiction: The Theory and Practice of Self-Conscious Fiction*. New Accents. London: Methuen, 1984.

————. *Practising Postmodernism, Reading Modernism*. London: Arnold, 1992.

White, Hayden. "The Value of Narrativity in the Representation of Reality." *Critical Inquiry* 7 (1980): 5-27.

————. *Tropics of Discourse: Essays in Cultural Criticism*. Baltimore: Johns Hopkins UP, 1978.

Williams, Nigel. *Star Turn*. London: Faber, 1985.

Winterson, Jeanette. *The Passion*. 1987. London: Penguin, 1988.

Woolf, Virginia. *The Common Reader*. London: Hogarth Press, 1951.

INDEX

ENGLISH LITERARY STUDIES publishes peer-reviewed monographs (usual length, 45,000-60,000 words) on the literatures written in English. The Series is open to a wide range of scholarly and critical methodologies, and it considers for publication bibliographies, scholarly editions, and historical and critical studies of significant authors, texts, and issues. ELS publishes two to five monographs annually.